MY BIT

A Lancashire Fusilier at War
1914–1918

GEORGE ASHURST

Edited by Richard Holmes

in association with Antony Bird

THE CROWOOD PRESS

First published in 1987 by
The Crowood Press
Ramsbury, Marlborough
Wiltshire SN8 2HE

Paperback edition 1988

British Library Cataloguing in Publication Data

Ashurst, George
My bit : a Lancashire fusilier at war 1914–18.
1. Great Britain. *Army. Lancashire Fusiliers* – History
2. World War, 1914–1918 – Personal narratives, British
I. Title II. Holmes, Richard, *1946–*
940.4'81'41   D547.L2/

ISBN 1-85223-012-6 (HB)
1-85223-199-8 (PB)

Acknowledgements

The publishers would like to thank the following
for their kind permission to reproduce the
photographs: 1 to 4, George Ashurst; 5, the
National Maritime Museum; 6 to 12, the Imperial
War Museum.

Typeset by Q-Set, Gloucester
Printed in Great Britain by Redwood Burn, Trowbridge

CONTENTS

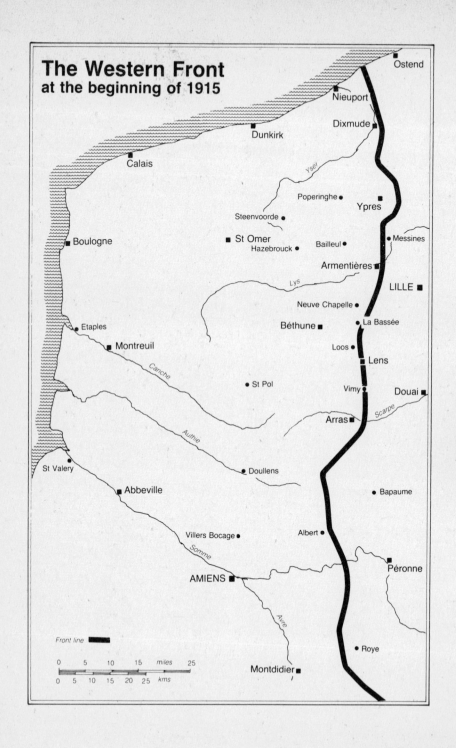

The Western Front
at the beginning of 1915

Ostend

Nieuport

Dixmude

Dunkirk

Calais

Yser

Poperinghe

Ypres

Steenvoorde

Messines

Boulogne

St Omer

Bailleul

Hazebrouck

Armentières

Lys

LILLE

Neuve Chapelle

Etaples

Béthune

La Bassée

Montreuil

Loos

Canche

Lens

St Pol

Vimy

Douai

Authie

Arras

Scarpe

St Valery

Doullens

Bapaume

Abbeville

Villers Bocage

Albert

Somme

Péronne

AMIENS

Avre

Front line

Roye

| 0 | 5 | 10 | 15 | *miles* | 25 |
| 0 | 5 | 10 | 15 | 20 | 25 | *kms* |

Montdidier

4

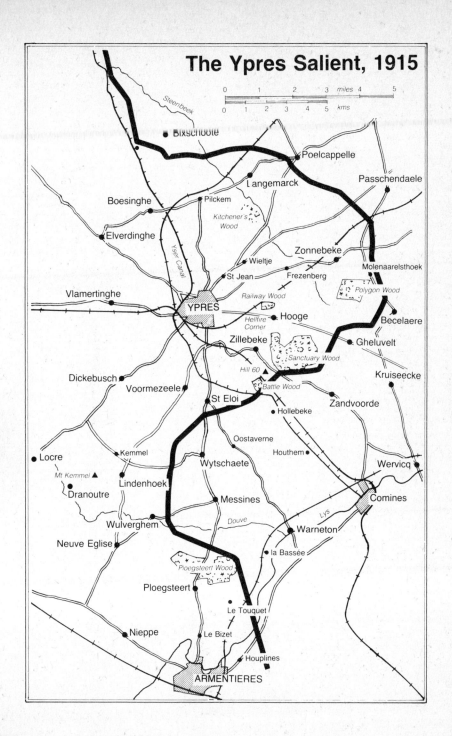

The Ypres Salient, 1915

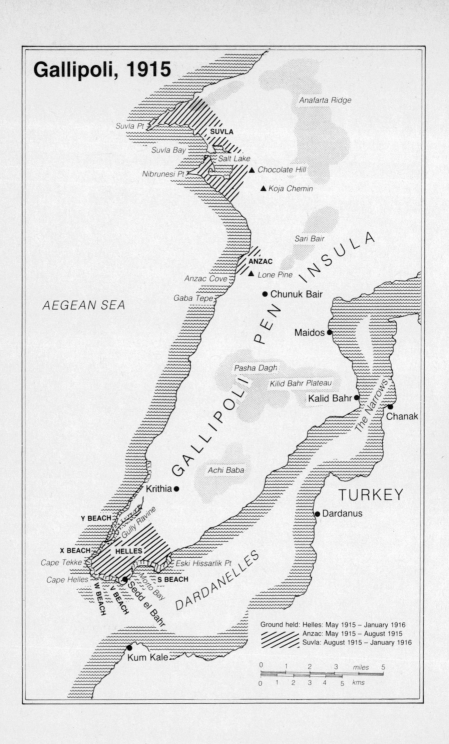

Gallipoli, 1915

Anafarta Ridge

Suvla Pt

SUVLA

Suvla Bay

Salt Lake

Nibrunesi Pt

▲ *Chocolate Hill*

▲ *Koja Chemin*

Sari Bair

ANZAC

Anzac Cove

▲ *Lone Pine*

Gaba Tepe

● **Chunuk Bair**

AEGEAN SEA

Maidos ●

Pasha Dagh

Kilid Bahr Plateau

Kalid Bahr ●

GALLIPOLI PEN INSULA

The Narrows

● **Chanak**

Achi Baba

Krithia ●

Y BEACH

Gully Ravine

X BEACH

Cape Tekke

HELLES

Eski Hissarlik Pt

Cape Helles

Morto Bay

S BEACH

W BEACH

V BEACH

Sedd el Bahr

TURKEY

● *Dardanus*

DARDANELLES

Kum Kale

Ground held: Helles: May 1915 – January 1916
Anzac: May 1915 – August 1915
Suvla: August 1915 – January 1916

| 0 | 1 | 2 | 3 | *miles* | 5 |

| 0 | 1 | 2 | 3 | 4 | 5 | *kms* |

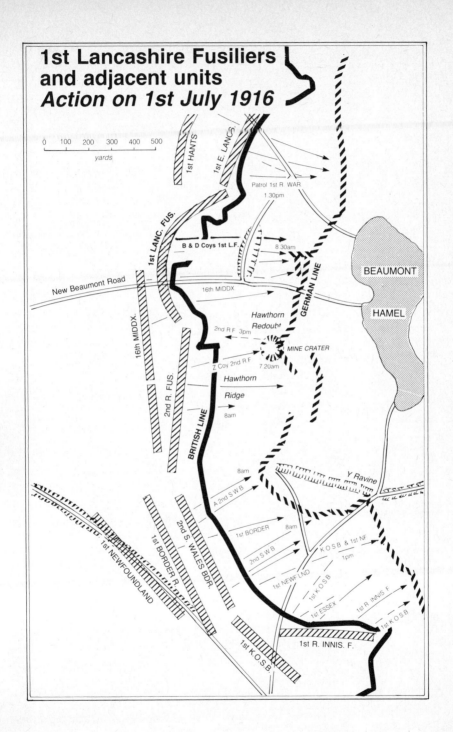

1st Lancashire Fusiliers and adjacent units
Action on 1st July 1916

0 100 200 300 400 500
yards

1st HANTS

1st E. LANCS

Patrol 1st R. WAR
1.30pm

1st LANC. FUS.

B & D Coys 1st L.F.   8.30am

BEAUMONT

New Beaumont Road

16th MIDDX

GERMAN LINE

HAMEL

Hawthorn
Redoubt

16th MIDDX.

2nd R.F. 3pm

MINE CRATER

2nd R. FUS.

Z Coy 2nd R.F.   7.20am

Hawthorn

Ridge

BRITISH LINE

8am

Y Ravine

8am

A 2nd S W B

2nd S. WALES BDR.

1st BORDER   8am

1st BORDER R.

2nd S W B

K O S B & 1st NF
1pm

1st NEWFOUNDLAND

1st NEWF'LND

1st K O S B

1st ESSEX   1st R. INNIS. F

1st K O S B

1st K.O.S.B.

1st R. INNIS. F.

7

INTRODUCTION

It is doubly surprising that George Ashurst has written of his service in the Lancashire Fusiliers during the First World War. In the first place, it is usually officers or middle-class men serving in the ranks – by preference or circumstance – who have left written accounts of their experiences. There are, it is true, several exceptions – most notably the marvellous Frank Richards – but it remains true to say that well observed first-hand accounts by working-class soldiers are relatively rare. And, as the opening chapter so clearly demonstrates, George Ashurst came from a working-class background typical of that of so many of the soldiers who fought in the First World War. Secondly, the odds against Ashurst surviving to write were almost impossibly high. The fortune of war put him in the path of a German gas attack at First Ypres, ashore on Gallipoli, and over the top on the first day of the Somme. Not only did he survive these pitched battles, but he also bore months of trench warfare across the whole length of the British sector of the Western Front, as well as in Gallipoli, and took part in a dozen or more grim and dangerous trench raids and patrols in no-man's-land. In the process he did indeed earn two 'Blighty ones' – but he was lucky not to share the fate of the 13,642 Lancashire Fusiliers who perished during the war.

George Ashurst wrote the bulk of his memoirs (though not the section dealing with his childhood and youth) from diary and memory in the 1920s. This fact has two important consequences. In the first place, Ashurst was often unaware of the accurate details of the events in which he participated. It is temptingly easy for historians to regard the first-hand accounts – written or oral – of survivors as the pure and undiluted truth. Such is rarely the case. Even when events are recalled shortly after they have happened, memory still plays tricks, with snatches of experience being collated in a haphazard order, like clips of film assembled at random from the cutting-room floor. There is a natural tendency for the mind to shut off the most ghastly episodes, and the stress of battle itself interposes a filter between an event and its observer. Lieutenant Geoffrey Malins, who filmed the British attack on Beaumont Hamel on the first day of the Somme, described the process well:

The noise was terrific. It was as if the earth were lifting bodily and crashing against some immovable object. The very heavens seemed to be falling. Thousands of things were happening at the same moment. The mind could not begin to grasp the barest margin of it all.

And there are other problems. Most front-line soldiers in most wars live on a diet of rumour intermixed with partly explained facts. During the First World War an understandable desire to preserve secrecy coupled with a tendency for information not to filter its way right down the chain of command to the non-commissioned ranks meant that private soldiers and NCOs (and, indeed, a good many officers) often had only the haziest idea of the progress of the war outside the narrow frontage of their own battalion – or even their own company. Rumour made up for the shortage of hard facts, and rumour often coalesced to assume the status of truth in the minds of survivors. Ashurst is consequently in error on several points of detail. He believed, for example, that the mine beneath the Hawthorn Redoubt was blown at 7.30 on the morning of 1 July 1916, and that its explosion was the signal for the assault. He also transposes his battalion's tour of duty in the Nieuport sector in 1917 with its time in the line north of Ypres in the winter of 1917–18. Ashurst could have corrected these facts by checking them against a regimental or official history, but in the process much of the freshness of his account might have disappeared. Moreover, what soldiers believed to be the case is often as interesting as the objective but bald fact which emerges from official records.

This caveat leads naturally on to the second consequence of the way in which Ashurst wrote. The attitudes he describes are essentially those of the working-class Englishman of sixty years ago. Authority was accepted instinctively, even when those wielding it were disliked. Ashurst's comrades complained frequently – as British soldiers tend to. They muttered when being given a pep talk by their divisional commander on the eve of the Somme, and gave vent to 'horrible wishes and curses' when pushed along on the march by 'the comfortably mounted adjutant'. But they kept going. Ashurst makes no secret of his contempt for shirking amongst the officers, but is always prepared to give credit where it is due: he describes 'one gallant young officer' trying to force panic-stricken men to stand and fight at the point of his revolver. He admired bravery wherever he saw it, and the picture of a signaller springing up onto the bank of the sunken road in front of Beaumont Hamel, only to fall back riddled with bullets, remained engraved on his memory.

Ashurst's comrades were certainly no angels. They drank to excess when the opportunity offered – many were the worse for drink when their battalion left the regimental depot for war. He describes a brothel in Armentières, its tables 'swimming in cognac and *vin blanc*', with a queue on the stairs, where 'the boys did their best to stand upright' when the padre arrived to rebuke them. Valuable items with no clearly identifiable owner were 'liberated'; Ashurst gives one lively description of the sergeants in his company carrying out a successful tomb-robbing raid by night.

Like so many front-line soldiers of the First World War, Ashurst reveals no particular hatred for his enemy. He was glad of the truce of Christmas 1914, and complains bitterly of 'the comfortably housed and well fed "Heads" in the rear' who 'started the war again'. The Germans are 'Fritz' and the Turks 'Johnny Turk', and there is no evidence of resentment towards either. Far from it: on one occasion, when burying 'a good-looking lad', he took care to place a photograph of the dead German's family next to his heart, and on another he and his comrades refrained from firing on a German who was 'too brave to die'. Nevertheless, Ashurst's lack of any feeling of personal antipathy did not prevent him from doing his duty. He got closer to the German front line than most of his comrades on 1 July 1916, and the frequency with which he was selected for patrols bears testimony to his fighting spirit. He was promoted steadily through the non-commissioned ranks, and was completing his training for a commission when the war ended.

Yet it was not lofty motives that kept him in the trenches; indeed, he admits that he might have considered malingering or desertion, but the former was foreign to his nature and the latter would have shocked his family. There were times when he clearly considered that he had 'done his bit', and on one occasion he told his company commander so in as many words. He was glad of his 'Blightly ones', and accepted the offer of a commission because he agreed with his men that 'it was a glorious opportunity . . . while I was away for my instruction the war might finish'. But there was an innate conviction that the allies must win; that 'sneaking away [from Suvla Bay] like a thief in the night' was wrong; that to 'hold on grimly, suffering heavy casualties but losing no ground' was the right way to behave.

It is in his dealings with non-Europeans that Ashurst's prejudices are most evident. He watched a group of mutinous Chinese labourers being rounded up, noting that 'if quiet had not reigned in that compound those Chinks would have been mown down like wheat. Perhaps this treatment looked a little harsh, but drastic treatment was necessary with this wild, uncivilised crowd.' He similarly makes no secret of his contempt for the 'dirty, lousy, unshaven' Greek labourers at Mudros or the 'grinning native' who stole his cigarette in Egypt.

In editing George Ashurst's memoirs I have made only minimal changes in the text, simply removing many of the inverted commas and capitals with which the original is so liberally seeded. Facts stand as Ashurst recalls them, and many French phrases are those of the British infantryman rather than the dictionary. I have used footnotes to throw more light on individuals or events and to indicate those occasions on which Ashurst's recollection and a more objective view of history differ, and have inserted passages in italics which put the events that Ashurst describes into their proper context. The text has been checked against

Introduction

Major-General J. C. Latter's excellent *History of the Lancashire Fusiliers 1914–1918* (2 volumes, Aldershot, 1949), and the appropriate volumes of the *History of the Great War, Based on Official Documents*. Where the two conflict, as they do over the layout of the 2nd Battalion's trenches at Mouse Trap Farm in May 1915, I tend to accept the evidence of the former. It is notable, however, that both histories gloss gently over events which Ashurst describes in harsh detail: his account of his company's precipitate (and, let it be said, by no means surprising) departure from the line at Mouse Trap Farm has little in common with the regimental history's description of men 'retiring'. The 1st Battalion's performance on 1 July 1916 is reconstructed from the battalion's War Diary (Public Record Office WO95/2300), and from Dr A. J. Peacock's useful work on 'The Sunken Road' in the occasional journal produced by the Western Front Association, *Gun Fire*, vol. 1, no. 3. Dr Peacock himself has been most helpful, as has Mr Bob Grundy, who drew my attention to these memoirs in the first place, and has provided the biographical note on George Ashurst.

In short, almost all of what follows is George Ashurst. Often he is frightened and uncertain, sometimes resentful that it is always the same men who are called upon to do the same dangerous jobs, occasionally infuriated by the fact that his discomforts were not shared by all ranks. He is usually ready for a cigarette or a glass of *vin blanc*, a game of Crown and Anchor and a sing-song. When gas drifts through the position and someone shouts 'Retire', he heeds the call without enquiring too closely into its origins. When his battalion attacks, he keeps going although logic and human nature suggest an early halt in a convenient shell-hole. He is proud to command a smart guard on divisional headquarters, happy to accept promotion, but not prepared to receive an unjust rebuke. His is the timeless voice from the ranks.

RICHARD HOLMES
Ropley, 1986

Dr Richard Holmes is a Senior Lecturer in the Department of War Studies at the Royal Military Academy, Sandhurst, and is also a Lt.-Col. in the Territorial Army. He is the author of numerous books on military history, most notably *The Firing Line* (1985) which has been extravagantly praised.

BIOGRAPHICAL NOTE

I came to know George Ashurst quite by chance in 1983, when I saw a small article about his war service in a local paper. I called to see him and found that he had written, as he says, 'a war book' – in fact a finely written manuscript of some fifty-six thousand words.

Reading the book through, I noticed with great interest that he referred to one of the most famous photographs of trench warfare, that of the Lancashire Fusiliers fixing bayonets, just prior to their attack on 1 July 1916 (IWM Q744). George mentioned that it was taken days before and, as he said to me, 'you could not move in that trench, it was so packed with men on 1 July'. This clarity of memory is not confined to remembering passages that he had written; indeed, he names a man on the left of the photograph as Corporal Holland, an 'old soldier'. At the close of the war George was at Ripon, Yorkshire, awaiting a commission. There he was kept on doing clerical work so that he could qualify for seven years' gratuity. Finally demobbed in January 1919, he went back to Wigan and Prescot Street Locomotive Depot. His job had been kept open for him but he was told to take a month's holiday and have a good time. This he did, spending most of his gratuity – and who can blame him, after what he had been through?

His return to civilian life meant being a fireman for the Lancashire & Yorkshire Railway Company. Odd hours of starting and finishing made for a difficult social life in the early twenties. In spite of this, George courted a girl from Platt Bridge, a few miles out of Wigan. Her name was Elizabeth Emily Joynson (Lizzie). On 7 April 1926 they were married at St James's Church, Poolstock, Wigan. A worse time to take a wife could not be found, as the General Strike started on 3 May and George was out of work – no strike pay, nothing.

Indeed, when the strike was over many railway men were told not to return to work until called for. Men were told to report for work in order of seniority and some of the younger railwaymen never got back to work at all. George started work again after eight weeks, a poor start to his married life. One year later, on 20 April 1927, their first child was born, Gladys Audrey. Later a tragedy struck them when a son, Geoffrey, was born, only to die when twelve days old.

Eventually, through a complicated railway procedure, he became a 'booked driver' – that is, he would only drive the locomotive and not be called upon to do fireman's duties. This job he retained until 1960, when he retired, being sixty-five years of age. He described life as a

12

railwayman in a privately printed book, *I want to be an Engine Driver,* by GASH, in the pseudonym of Bob Ashwood. One of George's pastimes is poetry and verse:

There she goes, so graceful, so fast.
A beautiful sight, as she hurtles past.
Near a hundred tons of shining steel
How weak and dwarfed she makes you feel.
Her powerful body, sleek, streamlined,
A machine created of man's mind.
Great long limbs, so lithe, so free,
A giant athlete she appears to be.
With strength of a thousand men,
Yet not the soul of one of them.
Not possessing an ounce of brain
Hauls five hundred tons of train.
Hungry monster with unquenchable thirst,
Devouring the miles, drinking to burst.
Running smoothly at terrific speed,
Faster than the Derby's winning steed.
Over junctions maze of shiny rail,
Charges like maddened harpooned whale.
Snorting out fire and white-hot breath,
Mimics the ancient dragon's death.
Speeding past yellow fields of corn,
Through wind and fog and wildest storm.
By lonely farm and cottage red,
Through town and city forges ahead.
Up barren hill, down leafy dale,
Her stamina sustains, does not fail.
On blackest night, or hottest day,
Her race is run on permanent way.
Acting quickly to her driver's will,
Paying tribute to engineer's skill.
This mighty engine driven by steam,
The fulfilment of James Watt's dream.
A wonderful descendant in metal,
Of her humble ancestor, 'The Kettle'.

In the early part of the Second World War George was asked to form, from the railway depot, a Home Guard unit, without uniforms, equipment or weapons – a body of about 50 men. Young and old would parade on Sunday morning for drill and PT under ex-Sergeant Ashurst. Eventually uniforms were forthcoming and rifles – wooden ones. Training was carried out at Central Park, the home of Wigan Rugby

Club. At this period weapons were in short supply but one rifle and 20 rounds found their way to George's unit for shooting practice. This was done on an old colliery tip, regulations being much more relaxed then than now.

After his official retirement George had a part-time job collecting for an Insurance Company. Without a car, this meant 'footslogging' to every customer – not that that was alien to him. After that, his last part-time job was at a local abattoir, working in the office. When the firm sold out, he also decided to finish as well, now being eighty years old – a fine working record.

It is surprising that after all the privations of that ghastly war and a hard life on a locomotive footplate George, in his ninety-second year, is in good health, despite suffering a heart attack at Christmas 1985. Whilst I have known him for a relatively short time he has become a pal. I can talk to him on nearly every subject and he has definite views on world matters. To me, George will never be an old man; he will always be a gentleman.

R. B. GRUNDY
June 1986

1

A Lancashire Lad

I was born on 3 March 1895 in the village of Tontine, a pleasant little place between Manchester and Liverpool. There were about twenty cottages, a beer house and a little Methodist church in the village. When I came into this world my parents already had three children, two girls and one boy.

We lived in an old two-bedroomed house in the middle of a row of houses. We had no modern amenities such as gas, electricity, bathroom, or flush toilet. The kitchen had a stone floor which was mopped and sanded – no oilcloth, carpets, or rugs – and at night the house was lit with paraffin lamps. The furniture consisted of a heavy wooden table, a set of drawers, and three or four heavy wooden chairs. In the back kitchen, fastened to the wall, there were shelves on which the plates and cups and saucers rested when not in use, and two or three hooks were driven into the wall to hold pots and pans, etc. Of course there was no fancy paper on the walls, just a few coats of whiting.

In the kitchen there was a huge iron grate with a hob on one side that held the big iron kettle, and a boiler on the other side of the fire, which burned wood or coal. The grate was black and polished with blacklead, and hot water was always to be had from the boiler. On bath night for the children a zinc bath was brought into the kitchen from the outside, where it hung on a nail driven into the wall. It was partly filled with hot water in which the children sat very uncomfortably to bath.

At the back of the house there was a small garden, big enough to grow a few potatoes, lettuce, cabbages and rhubarb.

We were a poor family. My father worked at a stone quarry about a mile from the village, and his wages were rather poor. To make things worse, he kept half of his wages for himself and spent them at the village pub.

My mother took in other people's washing to help pay the family budget, and was beaten every Saturday night by my drunken father for her trouble. She baked all our bread, kneading the flour and yeast in a huge 'pan mug', then placing it near the fire covered with a towel for the dough to rise. She baked the loaves of bread in tins, but specially for my father she had to bake 'cobs' on the oven bottom shelf. Of course during the week she would bake custard pies, apple pies and currant cakes, besides huge 'barm cakes' which the children loved, covered in black treacle or golden syrup, and oatmeal for breakfast covered in sugar or treacle. We used to beg for the top cut off father's boiled egg.

Through my mother's untiring efforts we were never short of food or clothing. As a young woman she had worked for years at a clothing factory and could always fix us up with cast-offs given to her by neighbours. Of course we didn't have any pyjamas and slept in our little shirts on old iron beds on which were straw mattresses covered with cheap blankets and any old coats that were available to keep us warm in winter. As soon as I could walk about I had to wear a pair of clogs, but I had a pair of child's slippers to wear on a Sunday to go to chapel with my elder brother and sisters.

Of course I don't remember much of my baby days, but something that stands out in my memory quite plainly is what happened on Saturday nights when I stood with my brother and sisters in our shirts on top of the stairs, crying and listening to my drunken father beating my poor mother black and blue, and there was nothing we could do about it.

As I got older it came time for me to go to school. My brother and sisters took me on the first day to a very old school about a mile from home, called Hallgates School. I didn't mind going to school at all except in the winter time, when it was foggy, snowing and cold. There were no school buses in those days, one slipped and trudged through the sludge.

It came my turn as I got older to take my father's fresh-cooked breakfast to the quarry before I went to school, and also the breakfast of the man who lived next door. His wife was a very nice lady and always gave me a thick slice of bread which had been dipped in the bacon fat at the bottom of the Dutch oven in which she had cooked her husband's eggs and bacon – a tasty bit I thoroughly enjoyed as I trotted off to the quarry.

Each Sunday morning I had to make a trip to the parish church of Upholland, not very far from the village, where I had to see the verger in the vestry and get two loaves of bread from him to take to a very old couple in my village.

Everyone in our little village knew every other person in the village, and I would say each other's business too. Every door was always open to a neighbour, and if anyone required help it was quickly and generously given. The little pub with its cheap, good beer and its domino table was the main recreation and entertainment for most of the men, while the women and children enjoyed their evenings at the little Methodist chapel.

Of course there was no radio, television or cinema, and almost no newspapers. Very often on the winter nights neighbours got together in one house, gossiping, having a sing-song, or playing parlour games. They weren't troubled about ruining posh furniture and carpets; there were none to spoil. They sat around on anything anywhere, eating sandwiches and drinking tea until it was time to retire to their own homes.

The country around the village in the summer time was beautiful and unspoiled by either people or machines. One could indulge in a long walk through the glorious fields, the silence broken only by the song of the birds or the gentle breeze through the magnificent trees. During school holidays I, along with other village boys, would set off early in the morning with a big bag of bread and jam sandwiches and a bottle of water – or, if lucky, a bottle of home made ginger beer made from nettles, dandelion, burdock, and meadowsweet. The whole day we would wander over the fields and into the woods, jumping ditches, climbing trees, chasing hares and pheasants, and bird-nesting, as happy and carefree as the day was long, trotting home at night tired out and as hungry as a pack of wolves. Then to bed, to sleep the sleep of an untroubled mind and a worn out body.

My father was a drunkard. He never went to church and was not concerned at all about religion. He never hit any of his children; my mother had to do the smacking when any of us was naughty. Still, he never objected to my mother and the children going to church so my mother saw to it that we learned about the Bible and Jesus Christ, and made us go to church twice on Sundays. Practically all our entertainment emanated from the little Methodist chapel, the children thoroughly enjoying the concerts and parties, especially at harvest time, when there was plenty of fruit on show, and at Christmas, when we received little presents and pretty cards.

In those days there was no flying off to the Continent or even going by train for a week at the seaside. In fact I only remember one occasion when I visited the seaside. The children were packed on to a wagonette drawn by one horse. It was a beautiful summer's day, and we all carried huge packets of sandwiches, fruit and cakes, along with sweets and pop – our destination the sandhills at Southport. We laughed and sang as the old horse trotted along.

At one place on the journey the road went over an old bridge across the canal. We all had to get down off the wagonette to help the horse pull it up the steep gradient. On arrival at Southport it was our first sight of the sea, and we played about on the sands until we were exhausted. It was a glorious time and we all thoroughly enjoyed ourselves. Getting back on the wagonette for the return journey we were so happy, but very tired, and it was a long ride back. We sang the songs we had learned at the little chapel until the rhythmic clop-clop of the old horse's shoes on the road lulled most of us to sleep long before we reached home.

On odd weekends my father would take me with him on a fishing trip to Abbey Lakes, a private estate not far from our village. To be allowed to get in the estate and fish my father had to pay twopence at the lodge gate. The grounds were beautiful with flowers and trees, and the lake in which we fished was thick with water lilies. In the middle of it was a pretty little island where lovely white swans nested, so that we had to be very careful with our fishing lines as they majestically swam by. There were no really big fish in the lake but we caught a few roach and perch. After a couple of hours we packed up our fishing gear and left the lovely estate, making our way home to dinner, which consisted of some chips and a fried perch.

Another incident that stuck in my childish memory was the day my grandma and grandad came to our house from Pimbo Lane, a village a couple of miles away from Tontine. My grandad was six feet tall; he had grey hair and a bushy grey moustache. He was wearing a black billy cap (bowler hat) tipped a little to one side on his head, a black suit, and a heavy silver chain hanging from his waistcoat pocket, in which he kept his watch. He was a real gentleman to me and he spoke in a soft, posh voice that I loved to hear, not at all like an ordinary railway platelayer which he was. My grandma wore a little close-fitting black bonnet with the ribbons tied under her chin and a black cape round her shoulders edged with lace.

My grandad was carrying a long, heavy wooden box. He opened it to show my mother and father, and I got a peep too. In the box was a man's long leg. It was my uncle Jack's leg and they were taking it to the churchyard to bury it. My uncle Jack worked at a brickworks in the village of Pimbo Lane; it was his job to work with the locomotives, taking loaded wagons of bricks to the railway sidings across the village lane. The engine always pushed the wagons in front of it and uncle Jack had to ride on the first wagon.

One day, as the train approached the village lane, uncle Jack noticed children playing on the line. He could not signal to the driver to stop because the train was on a curve and he was out of sight, so uncle Jack quickly jumped down from the wagon and ran as fast as he could to the children, throwing them clear of the path of the wagons. Bravely he had saved the children, but unfortunately one of his legs was caught by the wagon wheels and had to be amputated.

The quarry where my father worked closed down and he was out of work. Whatever my father was he was not lazy, and very soon he got a job down a coal mine. But it was too far away to travel to work each day so we had to move from the village. We got a cottage nearer to his work at a place called Bryn, a mile or so from Ashton-in-Makerfield, quite a fair-sized little town. The new house was much bigger than the cottage we had left, and it had gas light in it with the mantles on.

I and my brother and sisters had to go to a fresh school and church not very far from home. To me there seemed a lot more people, and life was a lot busier at Bryn. The electric trolly trams ran through Bryn on to Ashton-in-Makerfield from Wigan. The lads used to jump on the back step of the trams, gripping the handrail and having a ride while the conductor was collecting the fares inside.

Opposite our house, in the fields, was a farm where I spent a lot of my spare time. In the farmyard there was a huge boiler in which potatoes, cabbages and turnips were boiled, and I would keep the boiler stoked up until all the vegetables were nicely cooked. Then with a bucket I would feed the pigs, sometimes eating a potato myself because it was all very good food. Very often I would return home with a bag of potatoes, vegetables and eggs the farmer gave me for my help.

Every Friday night the children were allowed to stay up a little later than usual because on that night Chippy Bill, in his white apron and ringing his bell, would drive into the lane with his horse-drawn mobile chip cart. There was no chip shop in the lane and everybody seemed to wait for Chippy Bill. Of course we could make chips of our own, but there was something special about Chippy Bill's. We would hang around the cart watching him put potatoes under his chipper to drop in a tin as chips; then he would bend down and, opening the firehole door under his boiler, he would grab his little shovel and put a few nuts of coal on to the fire, the flames sometimes rising out from the top of the chimney peeping out above the roof of his cart.

We didn't have a long stay at Bryn. We were just about getting used to the place and everybody. My elder brother got married and left us and my sisters started work in a cotton mill at Wigan, having to travel by train and get up very early in the morning. Anyhow, once again a change of environment was on the cards.

My father got out of the mine and started to work at an iron foundry in Wigan. He also succeeded in getting a brand-new terraced house in Wigan, quite near the famous Wigan Pier. The house had a small front garden and a big back yard. It was fitted with gas lights in every room and we had an outside flush toilet. Of course once again it meant going to a fresh school and church, and our family had grown: there was Mother and Dad and six children, two of them working, so we were not quite so badly off now.

For myself, I found the town boys rather different from the country boys: they were more forward and lacked discipline and respect. I saw that it was far easier to get into serious trouble, especially with the police. Petty thieving was a regular pastime, and if one did not take part and concur with the gang one's life was made miserably lonely. Distracting a shopkeeper's attention while another of the gang helped himself was an easy game.

Nearby, the main road ran across a bridge over the canal. The gradient was rather steep and the horse-drawn vehicles going over it with a heavy load could only do it at a walking pace. Brewery lorries were a special and easy target for the boys. While the driver concentrated on his horses one of the boys would climb up the back of the lorry, reach over the backboard and hand down bottle after bottle to the fellows running behind. Then we would scamper off in the darkness and enjoy the spoils.

Once an ice-cream vendor left his handcart in front of a pub while he went in for a drink. While one of the lads kept a look-out the others emptied the biscuit tin into their pockets and then filled the tin with ice cream from the tub, quickly vanishing into the fields to devour it.

In the evenings we played all the dirty tricks one could think of just for fun, such as tying a long piece of black cotton to a coin with a hole in it, then throwing it down near the feet of someone passing by on the footpath and drawing it away again as the person began to look around thinking someone had dropped a coin; or tying the handle of a front door to the handle of the next door with a long piece of rope, then knocking at both doors and running off in the darkness as fast as we could. Other tricks were removing garden plant pots from one garden and placing them in a garden lower down the road; or getting a small box and filling it with dog's excreta and any other muck we saw lying around, then parcelling it up so nice and neat and placing it on the pavement and keeping out of sight to enjoy a good giggle as some person, glancing guiltily around, quickly picked it up, stuffed it under his coat and hurried off home.

Of course gambling on the cards was a must amongst the gang. If we had any money at all it had to go on the cards. We were big boys then and we could make a little pocket money doing all sorts of odd jobs besides the little spending money our parents allowed us. Sat out in the fields, or in any place at all where we could deal out the pack, we played three-card brag, often till late at night.

Soon most of the gang were doing part-time work. I was going the rounds with a milkman each morning before school, knocking on doors and pouring my pints and gills of milk into the jugs left on the doorsteps. In those days milk was delivered on a horse-drawn milk float, with large kits of milk from which the milkman measured his pints and gills. It was a terrible job in winter.

I must have been a decent scholar because one whole year before I was of age to leave school I had passed all exams and learned everything they could teach me, so my headmaster told me, and he gave me a job filling ink pots and running errands wherever they were needed. One nice errand I liked doing was carrying love letters from a teacher at my school to another teacher at a school the other side of town. They provided my train fare and usually tipped me as well.

The year soon passed and my schooldays were over, and it was time to find a regular job. I had not been idle long when my headmaster sent for

me. He said to me, 'Now, boy, have you got a job yet?' I said, 'No, Sir.'
He said, 'Now, look here, take this letter to Douglas Bank Colliery in
Woodhouse Lane and give it to the manager. I am recommending you to
him as an office boy, and good luck to you.'

I thanked him and off I went to the colliery office, and was taken into
the manager's office. After sending for the cashier to read what the letter
said, the manager turned to me and said, 'Well, my boy, after reading
this letter from your schoolmaster I can hardly refuse you the job, so you
can start work next Monday morning in the office. You will report to Mr
Barnes, the head clerk.' I thanked him and rushed off home to tell my
parents. My mother and father felt rather proud that I was starting work
with a collar and tie on, in an office.

I liked the work too and got on well with the other clerks. Very soon I
was doing accounts like the other clerks in the office. Then I was given a
job of paying out the miners' wages on a Friday afternoon. The wages
sheets were split up, one clerk paying the South Pit men out, another
clerk paying all the surface hands. I paid the men of the North Pit.
Spread out on my desk, quite easy to handle, was approximately £600.
The money was laid out in long heaps of golden sovereigns, half-
sovereigns, five-shilling pieces, four-shilling pieces, half-crowns, two-
shilling pieces, shillings, sixpences, threepenny pieces, and coppers,
then next to them were my pay sheets with the miner's name and
number and the wages he was entitled to. There were a couple of wooden
trays with small, round tin boxes, also numbered with the miner's
number. The balance on the pay sheets coincided with the balance of my
cash, which proved that I had dished out the wages correctly.

Even then I did have miners coming back with their wages and
claiming they had been paid £1 short. Of course one had to report it to
the cashier and it was usually paid, but the cashier put a stop to the
miners' little game. He said that the men, seeing that I was young and
new, had taken advantage of that knowledge, so he made a rule that
every man must check the wages in the tin before leaving the pay office.

My own wage was twelve shillings and sixpence a week. Of course
there were contractors down the pits, men who controlled about twenty
men or so with their work, and these contractors were paid the whole of
the wages earned by their men, and then paid out the wages to each
individual. The contractors required quite a lot of change in the wages to
do this, so I saw that they got this, and I was usually rewarded with half a
crown. I also made a little money running errands for the other clerks in
the office.

I had to walk to work and home again each night, and it was quite a
long way. I couldn't afford a bike, but one of the clerks in the office was
rather consumptive and his parents bought him a bike, thinking it would
get him out into the fresh air after working in the office all day. But he

found that riding the bike was too strenuous for him, so he generously offered the bike to me very cheaply. It was a brand new Royal Ajax and I was delighted. I could ride to work now and most of my pals also had bikes. I paid him two shillings and sixpence a week until I had paid for it.

During the evenings and weekends my pals and I would set off on our bikes through the country, wiping off mile after mile and enjoying every minute of it. During one of those trips we came across a bunch of boys firing a revolver at birds. We stopped to watch and I asked the owner if he would sell it to me for five shillings. He said 'Done' and gave me the gun – a six-chambered Bulldog – along with two bullets he had left. He also told me the name of a hardware dealer's shop in town where I could buy more bullets.

Some days later I ventured into the shop and asked for fifty bullets, telling the shopkeeper that my father had the gun. After a little hesitation he took my one shilling and ninepence, telling me to let no one see them until I got home. I fired a lot of bullets out of that gun, shooting at all sorts of things to test my aim, and also letting my pals have a go too.

One evening we were in the fields shooting away when three boys rode up on bikes and stopped to watch. They started to make fun and laugh at us. I told them to hop it and as they rode away one of them said that I couldn't hit a bull in an entry. Quickly I pointed the gun in his direction and pulled the trigger, aiming for his back tyre. Anyway I missed everything and only thought afterwards how easily I could have put a bullet into that lad's back.

Another time we were using the gun on some waste ground in front of a row of cottages. We struck a piece of paper on a telegraph pole and I took aim and fired. The next moment we heard a shattering of glass. I hadn't thought about the houses behind the pole if I missed it. Anyhow, as we saw a women come out of one of the cottages and look up at her bedroom window we vanished quickly.

While we were in the fields one day shooting the gun two men came up to us and and one asked me to let them have a look at it and try it. So I stuck a penny up in the ground about twenty feet away and let him fire at it. The bullet made the dirt fly two or three feet from the penny, but he seemed quite pleased with his shot and said, 'I'll give you ten shillings for the gun.' 'It's yours,' I said and took the ten shillings, having made a profit of five shillings on the deal.

The fever of guns had got hold of me now and when one of my pals told me about a fellow with one for sale we went off to see him. He had a beautiful six-chambered Smith & Wesson, the kind of gun which throws out the empty cartridges from the chambers all at once when you break it. He wanted half a quid for it. I paid him, and once more I was in possession of a very efficient revolver. Of course I always kept it hidden from my parents, except on one occasion. It was Saturday night, and my elder sisters were out. My drunken father came home shouting and cursing and beating my mother. I and the other children were standing on top of the stairs in our night clothes, crying and afraid. Suddenly I ran and got my gun and, rushing at my father, I fired the gun over his head saying, 'I'll bloody well kill you.' He was absolutely stunned and sat down on a chair as white as a ghost. He kept quiet the rest of the night. In the roof above his head was a bullet hole that remained there for years and, strange as it may seem, no one ever seemed to mention it again. That did not stop my father from his Saturday night madness, but I swore that when I was big enough I would beat him up for it.

He would not have us calling him and my mother Mum and Dad; it had to be Mother and Father. Mind you, my father could neither read nor write yet he could point out the racehorses he wanted to back in the sporting press. I or someone else wrote the bet out for him, and if his horses won, no matter at what odds, he knew how much money he had to draw from the bookmakers.

Since moving to Wigan I had learned a lot about people and life. In the town was a cinema, theatre and Hippodrome where the lads spent most of their Saturday nights. I paid threepence to go in the pit at the Hippodrome. Another threepence bought me a meat and potato pie and a bottle of pop. The entertainment was usually good and lasted from 7 to 11 p.m., with an interval of fifteen minutes when one could get a pass-out check to have a little walk out in the fresh air.

It was often said that if the variety artists passed all right at the Monday afternoon performance at the Wigan Hippodrome they were good for all week and would pass with any other audience in England. One week we had Charlie Chaplin in the show. Also there were brilliant Japanese acrobats and Chinese conjurers and magicians.

At the town's theatre we got musical comedies and thrilling dramas such as *The Face at the Window, The Man in the Iron Mask*, etc. After the show we had to walk home, there being no transport at that time of the night. We passed butchers' shops auctioning their last pieces of beef, people getting a nice piece of roast for a tanner (sixpence) or a nice lump of stewing beef for threepence; or we would stop and watch the police fighting and arresting the drunks, and have a good laugh as we saw a drunk wheeling another drunk on a barrow to the police station, with a policeman walking beside them.

As we left the town, walking home were scores of other people – couples arm in arm, gangs of young people prancing about, laughing, singing with a concertina, playing marches or the latest songs ringing out on the night air. Today that same road out of town is absolutely deserted except for motor vehicles.

On Sunday night everyone in their Sunday best would turn out if the weather was nice to patrol Wigan Lane, the main road from Wigan to Preston, a road on which most of the posh people of Wigan lived – along past Mabs Cross, the Plantation Gates, the Cherry Garden Inn, the Boar's Head Inn and on to Standish village. Couples arm in arm, fathers and mothers and children, groups of boys and girls strolled along talking, laughing and singing – hundreds of them. Today that road is practically silent on Sunday night except, of course, for the rush and swish of combustion engines.

Of course most of our leisure time was spent on our bikes, weather permitting. We went on trips to Southport and Liverpool and as far as Blackpool. Some evenings we raced each other on the main roads at breakneck speeds to see who was the fastest rider, until the police told us to stop our mad capers on the highway.

Life didn't seem too bad for me in those days. I had a nice job that I liked, a good bike to ride about on and go places, and a little money in my pocket.

Alas, all good things must come to an end. The owners of the colliery where I worked decided to close it down. The miners all finished but the office staff were kept on for another two months or so until the whole place was sold and cleared away. Of course I had to find other work. I managed to find jobs all right but my father would not let me start at them. He said, 'You have started work with a collar and tie on and you are going to keep it on, and if you start on any of these other jobs I will break your bloody neck.'

Of course it was not very easy to get a clerk's job at that time. It wasn't my fault that I was out of work so I wasn't too worried, and my mother took good care that I had a little spending money at the weekends. However, one day I came home for tea and it was something I did not like so I asked my mother if I could have something else. My elder sisters were having tea, and looking at me they said, 'Listen to him ordering a special tea, and out of work!' That really went home to me, and they little knew how much they had hurt me, but they were very soon to know.

I was already fed up with being out of work and getting jobs and not being able to take them on. So the next day, without saying a word to anyone, I made my way round to the recruiting sergeant's office in town. While I was standing in front of the place a young fellow came up to me and asked was I going to join up. I said yes. 'Come on then, let's go in,' he said.

The recruiting sergeant spoke to the other fellow first and then he turned to me and asked how old I was. I told him I was sixteen and a half years. He said, 'No, you are seventeen and a half. You are mistaken.' 'No, I am not,' I said. 'Oh yes, I am booking you down as seventeen like your pal here. How long do you want to sign up for?' We both said 'Seven years, Sir.' But he said, 'When you get in the army you might not like it, so I will tell you what to do. Join the Special Reserve, which means that you will do six months in the barracks and seven years on the reserve, with just a month's camp every year.' We thought that would be best. 'All right,' he said, report here to me tomorrow afternoon at 3.30 p.m.'

Without saying anything at all to my parents I was at the sergeant's office on time and the other fellow was waiting for me. The sergeant came out to us and said, 'Come on', and we walked along with him to a magistrate in town. We each held a bible in our hands, repeating what the magistrate read out to us, and we were sworn in.

As we walked back again to the sergeant's office I was thinking seriously of what I had sworn to do on oath, but I knew in my heart that I never would stick to that oath. Anyway, we arrived back at the recruiting sergeant's office and he gave us one shilling and ninepence each and a railway warrant to Wellington Barracks at Bury.

We had both joined the Lancashire Fusiliers Special Reserve. That meant doing six months in the barracks and one month's training in camp each year for seven years.[1]

On arriving at the barracks we were taken by the sergeant of the guard to a long wooden hut with a stove, forms and wooden beds with straw palliasses. A couple of army blankets were thrown at us and we were told to present ourselves at the barrack dining-halls with the troops at meal times until Monday morning, when we would be given our full soldiers' clothes and kit.

I soon learned what life was like in the army and that it paid to do as one was told smartly and quickly. At meal times there was no menu to choose from. What it did say on the menu was what you got, whether you liked it or not, and one serving only. If you didn't like the dripping you got with your bread for tea you bought a twopenny pat of butter at the canteen.

There were two companies of soldiers in the barracks, G Company and H Company. The lad I enlisted with was put into G Company and I was put into H Company. Still, we could meet very often when off duty in the barracks.

I got on very well as a soldier, except for little reminders by the sergeant-major that I was a soldier now and 'Take your hands out of your pockets, stick your chest out and your chin in' as I walked across the barrack square. I felt really fit, too, with the cross-country running and the gym exercises we had daily, and I loved the musketry lessons and the shooting on the firing range with the ·22 rifles.

There was also a school and a teacher in the barracks where one could go in the afternoon and sit at desks with pen and paper to improve one's education. There were examinations, and we could get a third-class certificate. If you were also a first-class shot with the rifle you got sixpence a day on your pay. I got my third-class certificate and my second-class certificate as well. There were quite a lot of rather ignorant fellows in the army at that time, whereas I was straight out of an office.

I also had a taste of what it was like to be in trouble in the army. Three fellows and myself were caught by the orderly sergeant playing cards after lights-out. We appeared before the CO and pleaded guilty. He sentenced us to ninety hours' detention. We were put separately into cold stone cells with a hard wooden bed and pillow and, a little iron-barred window that let the cold in and kept most of the light out.

Every morning we were awakened at 5 a.m. by the sergeant of the guard. 'Get out of it and empty the latrine bucket, swill it out and polish it. Get clean water and mop out the cell and the passage outside. Get the food tin and go to the cookhouse for porridge and tea to eat in the cell. No smoking allowed.' All cigarettes were taken from us. After polishing the food tins we gave our boots a good shine, put on the full fighting kit of an infantryman, picked up a rifle and marched out smartly onto the barrack square. Then two hours' marching up and down and round about the square. Back again inside the cells we sat almost exhausted, giving the rifle a good cleaning and oiling. Another trip to the cookhouse and once again the cleaning and polishing of food tins, which shone like silver.

If the afternoon was fine we turned out in our gym kit, doing all sorts of exercises, and then back again inside to clean and blanco all our equipment. Each day we followed the same rigmarole and then we were locked up in the cold cells until 5.0 a.m. The walls were so thick I couldn't hear what my mate was shouting in the next cell. It certainly made me keep to the straight and narrow path afterwards.

July came around and that was the month the battalion always went to camp. That year we moved out of Bury to Brackenber Moor, the wild country around Kendal. The weather was not bad at all and I thoroughly enjoyed the month under canvas, and the great open country was a nice change from Wellington Barracks. We did a lot of drill and route marching in full pack, attacking and defending hills. We also played lots of games and sports, competing against other units camping round about us. We were also allowed passes to visit towns and villages for entertainment in the evenings.

There was, of course, a firing range on which we did quite a lot of shooting. One day while we were shooting at a target 600 yards away, lying prone on the ground, the colonel came around to watch us. I was shooting at the end target, the colonel behind me. After my first shot the lads in the butts signalled me a bull. The colonel congratulated me and said, 'Carry on, boy.' I shot again and was signalled another bull. My next shot was an inner, and the next shot a bull again. My fifth shot was also a bull. The colonel was amazed and told me to stand up. He said, 'I have never seen such shooting in my life. Nineteen points out of a possible twenty, and by a recruit too. Here, take this, my boy', and he gave me five shillings. That shooting labelled me as a first-class shot.

One day we had a very heavy thunderstorm; the rain poured down. We were sat in our tent with the flap partly open, looking across the fields at a Royal Artillery battery who were also camped nearby. We could see the guns and a sentry walking about on guard over them with his rifle across his shoulder and with fixed bayonet. Suddenly a terrific flash of lightning seemed to strike down from the sky. There was a flash which appeared to come from the sentry and the next moment we could see him lying on the floor with other soldiers running towards him. The sentry was killed. We supplied a party of soldiers to attend his funeral.

When the camp at Brackenber Moor was over I had done my six months and I was due for discharge back into civilian life as a reservist for the next six years, with an obligation to attend for one month's training per year. As I was leaving the barracks for home the sergeant who had been my schoolteacher came to me. He begged me to sign on as a regular soldier and stay in the army. He said there was certain promotion for me and that I was making the biggest mistake of my life going back into civilian life. I have often wondered since if he was right. I rather think he was.

Anyhow, I had a few weeks of freedom from the strict discipline of the army but I had to do something for my keep so it was a case of looking for work again. My father was not so keen now on my finding a collar-and-tie job and I managed to get a job at the locomotive depot in the town. It was shift work, 6.0 a.m. to 6 p.m., twelve hours a day, and 6.0 p.m. to 6.0 a.m., twelve hours the following week, on nights. My wages were seventeen shillings per week. It was not hard work, yet interesting, cleaning those massive locomotives, along with lots of other young fellows.

The month of July came along and from the War Office came a letter telling me to report to Bury Barracks for my annual training. I reported there on the day and changed once again into army uniform. Very soon we were on our way to camp at Tenby in Wales, where we were under canvas quite close to the sea. In fact the firing range was on the beach. It was the same old camp routine. Cross-country marching in full fighting kit, gymnastic parades, sport and games, shooting on the range. Tenby was not a big place in those days so the troops preferred to go to Pembroke Dock for their enjoyment, a little further down the coast.

At this camp I was promoted to lance-corporal, the first step up the ladder for a soldier.

On 28 July the camp was over. We returned to Wellington Barracks and I was once more discharged into civilian life, going back to my job at the locomotive depot. I had only been back home a few days when I received a War Office letter ordering me to report at Wellington

Barracks on 8 August 1914 for active service. I showed the letter to my boss at work. He said, 'Well, lad, you will have to go, and I don't think it will be any picnic. But remember, whenever you do come back your job here will be always open for you. The best of luck.' We shook hands and said goodbye.

2

Going to the Wars

I duly presented myself at Bury Barracks. Crowds of people were outside the barracks. The public houses nearby were doing a roaring trade to both men and women. There was a lot of hand-shaking, kissing, and good wishes; women were crying and laughing and quite a number of men were drunk. Pushing my way through these people and past the sentry, who just stood and watched the crowd, I reported to the sergeant of the guard. In no time at all I was sent off to the doctor, and in less than twenty seconds I was marked fit for active duty abroad.

As I was dressing I heard commands being given to fall in for uniforms and fighting kit. These were thrown at us, along with a rifle, and I noticed with a thrill that my bayonet had been newly sharpened. They also threw at us a large piece of brown paper and some string to parcel up our civilian clothes. All was hustle in the barracks now and off we went to the gymnasium to change. In a few minutes we were looking like fighting men, and as I parcelled up my civilian clothes and labelled them for home I listened to jokes, curses and drunken singing. The next move was into the dining-hall for a meal of bread and cheese.

By about three o'clock in the afternoon the battalion was ready for moving off, with the exception of a few absentees, who were determined to get down as much beer as possible in case the next drink was a long time coming. We formed up on the barrack square and rather sloppily marched out through the gates. Outside the barracks was a big crowd of men, women and children. Some were cheering, some silent, and others crying. They broke into the ranks, kissing soldiers, shaking hands and wishing us the best of luck.

On we marched to the station, headed by the Bury Concertina Band playing popular songs and marches. Woman and children swung alongside, singing and cheering. On our arrival at the station the train was waiting. In we jumped and were soon rid of our heavy packs and hanging through the carriage windows. Eventually we drew out of the station, leaving the cheering crowds and the band playing 'Auld Lang Syne'.

Now we began to get settled, arranging our equipment so that we could be comfortable, and seeming to have time to think. The first topic of conversation was, of course, 'Where were we bound for?' No one had any idea; some of the boys had made enquiries, but had not found out our destination. Well, all we could do was to work out the direction the train was taking by noting towns and villages on the route.

There was an old African veteran or two in my compartment and I noticed a quiet calm about them.[2] They knew we were not going on any picnic. Other younger soldiers like myself suggested that the war might be over by Christmas. All along the line people cheered and children waved small flags. By now we were beginning to get our bearings; judging by the route we were travelling we were getting towards the east coast, and eventually our train drew into Paragon Station, Hull.

It was late in the evening as we formed up on the platform, and off we marched down to the docks, naturally expecting to board some ship and away to France. But that was not the case. Instead, we were packed into wharfs and sheds like sardines, and told to make ourselves as comfortable as we could. That night we tasted our first bit of active service. We had neither blankets nor bedding of any description, and had to settle down on the cold floor with our equipment, as best we could, with just our greatcoats to keep out the cold night air. Of course the night was spent smoking, shivering, swearing and uttering kind wishes on those responsible for our comfort. Some men managed to get a few hours sleep, under the influence of the beer they had swallowed during the day. Anyhow, morning came and not many needed calling twice.

We again fell in by companies, and marched off into town. Billets had been secured for us and my company halted outside a building called Wellington Rooms in Beverley Road, a kind of dance and concert hall. In this place we were very comfortable, arranging our own concerts and showing how we could dance with our heavy army boots on the beautifully polished dance floor. Food was very good and we got plenty of it, gifts of fruit and chocolates and cigarettes coming in daily from the townspeople as well as lots of books and magazines, which were very much appreciated by the boys, especially as we were confined to billets after parades. This confinement did not please the boys. They were continually breaking out of billets and absenting themselves, so the commanding officer decided to give us two hours liberty in the evening from 7 to 9 p.m.

While billeted here the parades and training was very stiff. The civilians used to stand by and watch us drilling. Our company commander, whose name was Lyle, was rather stern, giving his commands rather fiercely, and insisting on every movement being made perfectly.[3] The women standing by and watching, as usual in sympathy with Tommy, suspecting that our commander was Lyle of the famous syrup firm said that in future their children would eat nothing but black treacle.

During our stay in these rooms I was rather fortunate, being given the post of sanitary corporal, having two men under me and being responsible for the cleanliness of the billet. Of course we were excused all parades, and we had a fairly easy time of it.

We carried on here for about three weeks, and then came orders to move; so, saying goodbye to our friends in Hull, we moved off to Paull Battery. This was a small fort at the mouth of the Humber. Here we were kept busy digging trenches and putting barbed wire round the fort. We also supplied the guards for the searchlights. These searchlights were in a kind of dug-out, on the bank of the river in front of the fort. The beam of light shone out across the surface of the river to the opposite bank, so that not even the smallest boat could come up the river without being seen. The light also traversed from left to right through about 45 degrees, and was controlled by the gunners in the fort behind, so that when a ship came into the light it could be seen as plainly as in daylight for quite a few minutes.

Sometimes a little excitement would be caused. A gun in the fort behind would boom out and a shell would throw up the water in front of a ship coming up the river. This, I believe, was when a ship was not showing the proper flag signal, because it usually caused a scurrying of sailors and a rearrangement of flags on the boat. During the night guard one could watch the rats darting hither and thither on the river bank.

Life was a little easier here, and now and again rumours would fly about that some spy had been caught prowling around the fort. One could not get leave from the fort, and it was also very hard for friends or relatives to get to there. All roads to the fort were guarded by troops and military police, and anyone approaching had to undergo a searching examination. Then orders came again to move back to our billets in the town. Everyone was glad of this, and we were soon comfortable again and back with our friends, but this time a new parade was started, and a very nasty one too. Every evening at 9.30 every man in the billet had to dress in full fighting kit and fall in ready to march off to the station. We would have a roll call and away to the station, just to march back again to the billet. This parade was called a practice alarm. The boys said it was just to kid old Fritz that we were sending over troops in thousands.

Once again we got orders to move, and this time our destination was Sutton, a village just outside Hull. Here we were billeted in a school and barns. Our training here was even harder than ever it had been, and our liberty absolutely nil. We were confined to the village, and the only public house was put out of bounds. This certainly did not go down very well with the boys and there was a lot of crime, the boys breaking out of the village and some not coming back at all. Others volunteered for active service and asked to be put on drafts for the front, preferring the dangers of France to the hard training and strict routine in the village.

During my stay here I tore my left hand on a barbed-wire entanglement, through which we were practising an attack. The wire was rusty and soon I was raving with blood poison. After a sleepless night or two I was sent to the Naval Hospital at Hull. Friends of mine in Hull came to see me, bringing me most things I required, and helping me to feel at home and forget my pain. Then, after having come close to losing my arm, I returned to Sutton quite fit and well again.

Batches of men were being sent off to France by now, almost weekly, and while I had been in hospital my best pal, Tom, had gone on a draft there. Men were actually clamouring to be put on drafts, they were so fed up with life at Sutton. I was also anxious to get away to France now that my pal Tom had gone, but my captain refused to send me. He said that I was of more use as an instructor and that he was going to recommend me to be promoted to full corporal. This meant more pay and of course an easier time, but I, like a lot more, wanted to see the real thing and told my captain so. After he had told me how big a fool I was, he decided to put me on a draft for the front.

About 29 November 1914 we entrained for Southampton. We settled down as comfortably as was possible under the circumstances and smoked and played cards practically the whole long journey. Arriving at Southampton we got off the train and went straight on the boat. She was a cattle-boat called the *Manchester Commerce*. The cattle stalls had been given an extra whitewashing and into these we were packed like sardines. Lifebelts were issued to us, with orders to wear them until we received orders to take them off. To make things a little exciting before we sailed, a soldier cut his throat on deck and had to be carried off the boat again, dying. To cheer us up some fellow put it out that the poor chap had been to France before.

Nothing exciting happened during our sail to Le Havre, which took the boat about six hours, two destroyers escorting us the whole way across. We anchored down outside Le Havre for a few more hours and then moved alongside the quay and disembarked, the French cheering us and wishing us 'bonne chance'. Then off we marched to the base camp, a distance of about four miles. The camp was right up on the heights, and up and up we went with our heavy equipment pulling us down, feeling just about ready to drop as we arrived at the base. We were met by old chums who had come on before us, and soon we learned what was in store for us.

The camp was under canvas and six inches deep in mud. Food was rotten and insufficient, Woodbine cigarettes were sixpence a packet, and one had to queue up for a packet even when they were to be got at all. Only one blanket per man was issued, and we had to keep warm at night by sharing each other's blankets and sleeping in our uniforms. Life was just terrible, the route marches were almost killing, and one was delighted to see one's name on the list of a draft for the front line.

My turn for the front soon came, and I was given extra ammunition and twenty-four hours' rations – consisting of bully beef and biscuits, tea and sugar – and away we marched to the station. Here we were packed into cattle-trucks to such an extent that we could only move about with difficulty on the top of equipment. We were too packed and cold to sleep, and we jolted along like this for sixteen hours, the French people cheering as we passed through the villages. We had not much interest in the scenery and really hardly noticed it, having to keep the van doors closed to keep warm.

We were all glad, and feeling rather stiff, when the train reached its destination. It was dark as we jumped out of the trucks and fell in to move off. Guides were waiting to take us to the battalion, and cheered us up a little by telling us that the battalion was at present resting out of the line. Eventually we moved off along those terrible uneven and dirty roads, with about seven miles of a march before us. As we marched along, rather stiffly from our cramped ride, we saw occasional flashes on the sky ahead of us and heard the distant rumble of guns. Now and again a star light would rise above some ridge and light up the surrounding country.

As I plodded on, simply following the shadows in front of me and listening to the squelch of marching feet in the mud, I tried to ease the pain in my shoulders caused by the straps of my heavy equipment and rifle, and my mind wandered a little. I wondered if I should be killed or wounded. I pictured my home in England with my parents and sisters and brothers grieving over my death, and I pictured them greeting me happily, home again with a lovely Blighty wound. I wondered what it must feel like to be hit with a bullet or stabbed with a bayonet.

Then I was brought back again to reality, with a little shouting in the ranks. We were approaching the village in which our regiment was resting, and some men had come a little way to meet us. Soon we marched into the village and came to a halt. The adjutant came along to detail us to our companies.

Ashurst had joined the 2nd Battalion the Lancashire Fusiliers. The battalion had arrived in France on 23 August 1914, and formed part of the 4th Division's 12th Infantry Brigade. It was heavily engaged in General Sir Horace Smith-Dorrien's stand at Le Cateau on 26 August, where it lost six officers and what the regimental history calls 'an uncertain number of NCOs and men' killed, 3 officers and 86 other ranks wounded, and 6 officers and 402 other ranks missing. Three officers and 143 other ranks subsequently rejoined. When Ashurst joined the battalion in November 1914 it was in billets at Le Bizet, a small village on the Franco-Belgian border near Armentières. During the period from November 1914 to April 1915 it spent from three to five days in billets with the same period in the line at Ploegsteert Wood or, more usually, Le Touquet. Major (later Brigadier-General) C. J. Griffin took over the battalion from Lieutenant-Colonel (later Lieutenant-General Sir) R. K. H. Butler on 28 November, when the latter was appointed to command 3rd Infantry Brigade.

Tom, my old pal, came along to greet me, and told me to get in his company if possible. I managed to do this and was detailed off to my billet, an estaminet.[4] Quickly getting rid of my heavy equipment, I settled down to a glass of French beer and a talk about things with Tom. I learned that the name of the village was Le Bizet, half French and half Belgian, and that it lay just to the left of Armentières and in rear of Le Touquet.

I asked Tom where I was to sleep, and he said, 'On the floor here, of course' – just under the counter. He told me of some friends of his in the village and took me round to see them. He soon introduced me, in his best French, telling them that I had come hundreds of miles that day and that I was hungry and tired. The coffee pot was soon put to use and Tom slipped round to the village butcher's, bringing back a couple of fine chops. In a few minutes I was enjoying a very welcome meal and beginning to think that life at the front was not bad after all. While making the chops disappear, Tom was telling me about the trenches and what was before me.

The troops had settled down to this kind of warfare now, after Fritz's retirement from Paris. My battalion was doing four days in and out of the trenches alternatively with the King's Own Royal Lancaster Regiment. Tom showed me his clothes, covered in clay from head to foot, and it was plain to see that he had been up to his knees in water. His rifle looked like a long stick of clay and, but for the breech cover, must have been useless.

Now and again the conversation would be interrupted for a moment by the rattle of the windows and doors of the cottage, as our guns just behind the village sent over a souvenir to Fritz.

Feeling much better after my supper, I suggested that we should get back to our billet. Tom motioned me to keep silent, and started a parley with his friends. Using his best French, he persuaded them to let me stop and sleep the night with him in a bed upstairs. After a few 'bonsoirs', Tom and I were comfortably tucked in a nice, soft, clean bed. My luck was certainly in on my first night at the front, and I just prayed that it would keep in.

Tom was soon snoring away, but I lay awake for some time, watching the flashes of the guns on the sky through the window, and listening to the bark of a machine gun as it traversed the enemy's parapet. I was thinking how pleased my parents would be if they could only know that I was so warm and comfortable. Eventually I fell off into a sound sleep, and was awakened by Tom the next morning, standing beside the bed and shouting, 'Coffee up.' I jumped up and dressed, sipping the hot coffee the while and feeling fine after a good night's rest. Downstairs to a hot breakfast of bacon and eggs, paid for, of course, with Tom's francs, and off we walked to our own billet.

There were no parades to speak of and the troops had really a very easy time of it. The parades were chiefly clothing and equipment inspection, kit inspection, pay, and baths. The troops spent most of their time in estaminets drinking *vin blanc* and French beer, playing cards, writing letters, and cleaning up generally.

During my first morning Tom told me that Fritz would shell the village in the afternoon, and sure enough he did. This appeared to be quite a regular occurrence, and almost at the same time each day. After dinner I got a little excited, waiting for the shelling to start and wondering what would happen. Soon we heard a bang in the distance, and for the first time in my life I heard the noise of a shell travelling through the air and coming in my direction. We were down in the cellar of our billet, but still I had the wind up, as more shells came screaming into the village and sent bricks and glass flying about.

When we thought he had finished shelling, Tom took me round to see the damage. One shell had gone clean into a house and killed two women and a soldier. The inside of the house was wrecked, and the poor people inside were blown to pieces amongst the bricks and wood and dust. The battalion ambulance men were doing their best to collect up the victims. The sight almost made me sick, but Tom began to help move the broken furniture and wrecked stairs, telling me that I would get more used to that sort of thing as time went on. The next couple of days passed over, writing letters and sipping *vin blanc*, the troops having as good a time as possible under the circumstances, Fritz not forgetting his part of the entertainment each afternoon.

With each issue of rations there were gloves, mitts, mufflers and socks sent over from the old country, the children in the village enjoying most of the fancy cakes and sweets sent over by sweethearts and mothers. I marvelled at the kiddies, who played in the village street as if they were thousands of miles from war, instead of being just outside the reach of rifle fire, playing their games until the guns of Fritz actually boomed in the distance, when they would scurry off down the cellar like frightened rabbits.

Then came the night for us to move up into the trenches. I noticed the men's spirits drop a little, and I was feeling excited and perhaps a little nervous. Dressed in my woolly sheepskin coat, with two big French loaves inside my heavy pack and my pouches bulging with ball ammunition, I felt quite a real fighting man. We formed up in platoons in the village street, had a roll call and marched off in the darkness, the villagers shouting after us, 'Bonsoir' and 'Bonne chance'. At first we marched along in fours, not in the usual smart way, and singing a popular song, but strangely quiet and often out of step. I noticed the star lights appear to be coming nearer and the crack of a rifle seemed much closer.

Then I heard a quiet order to halt; the troops fell out of the ranks and leaned about on their rifles or anything, to ease for a little while the weight of their packs. This halt was known as 'Smokers' Corner', because it was the spot where smoking had to cease on going into the trenches, and where smoking was permitted on leaving the trenches. After about ten minutes of resting and smoking, our officer said, 'Now boys, ready? Don't forget, no lights and as little noise as possible. Follow on.' This time we moved off in single file. The road now was very muddy, and I noticed a quickening of the pace.

On we went, filing on behind each other like shadows, slipping and sliding in the mud under our heavy loads, listening for a warning from the man in front to just miss a huge shell-hole half full of water, and passing the warning back to the struggling man behind you. On we went, sometimes doing a little run to keep in touch with the shadow in front, and, although it was the depth of winter, I was perspiring like a man in a Turkish bath.

Suddenly a star light would go flaring into the sky, lighting up everything around us. Down we would go on our knees and keep as still as statues, pushing forwards again the moment its light failed. Rifles and machine guns would keep on bursting out, and bullets came whistling over our heads, causing me to keep ducking down, the 'ping' of the bullet seeming to skim by my head. Now the crack of a rifle seemed to be quite near to us, and the shadows in front of me began to disappear. The boys were dropping into the trench, there being no steps in the slippery sides. We had to jump down or slide down into it. There was a lot of movement and whispering going on in the trench, a handing over of trench stores and a word about Fritz across the way, and the men we were relieving lost no time in assisting each other out of the trench and getting away as fast as possible.

We filed along the muddy trench, leaning on one side and then the other to keep our balance, the sergeant detailing us to our different posts. I was given a length of trench with three other men and placed in charge, seeing that I was a lance-corporal. Here we had to settle down in the depth of winter for four days and nights, until the very men we had just relieved came to relieve us again.

There was a little water in the bottom of the trench, but by chipping the sides of the trench and bailing out with an empty jam tin we could keep our feet something like dry. There was no way out of the trench except by climbing out, and cutting steps in the side with our entrenching tools. The next bit of trench on our left was almost flooded, causing us to have to dam up that end, and to get to the men on our left we had to get out on top, which, of course, could only be done in the night time.

My first night in the front line passed over very quickly. I was too windy to sleep, and also too cold. One man was on sentry for about one hour at a time. When not on sentry duty we passed the time cutting holes in the side of the trench, big enough to hold our bodies and rations, pegging our groundsheets to the trench side so that they would hang down over these holes. During a downpour of rain we could curl up in these holes, drawing our legs up after us under the groundsheet, and keep something like dry, so long as the pegs fastening the groundsheet would stick in the wet clay side.

Morning came after stand-to, a precaution that heralds the dawn in the front line.[5] We started to prepare breakfast, cutting pieces of wood into strips little larger than match sticks. Then we hung a mess tin on a peg stuck in the side of the trench and started a small fire under it, patiently feeding the fire with the little strips of wood, just keeping a flame burning and about as much heat as one would get from an ordinary paraffin lamp. All this trouble and patience was necessary because the smoke from a large fire is always a good mark for the enemy's artillery. By this long process we made a decent breakfast of tea and bacon, along with the French bread we had brought in with us.

After breakfast I wanted to have a look round and see what was in front of us, so I carefully peeped over the parapet to Fritz's lines. About five yards in front of our trench was one strand of barbed wire, a foot high from the ground, just fastened to staves driven into the soil, and on the barbs dangled empty jam and bully beef tins. The ground in front of the trench for a few yards was also sprinkled with these empty tins, and during the night rats prowling about looking for food would rattle the tins and cause the sentry to blaze away, wasting good ammunition. About two hundred yards in front I could see two rows of barbed wire and the earth thrown up immediately behind it. This I knew was Fritz's front line. Beyond that I could see a river, and on the farthest bank a small village, the houses broken and knocked about by our artillery.

After satisfying myself as to what the front looked like, I settled down under my groundsheet to have a little sleep. I slept quite soundly for a couple of hours and was awakened by one of my pals asking me to have some fried bully beef and biscuits. We were eating and talking and one of the boys named Brady, who like me was having his first day in the trenches, was on sentry. Then we heard the voice of our officer in the next trench, his voice raised as if angry at the sentry not being at his post. Brady also heard him and, knowing that in a moment the officer would be round the traverse and into our trench, he did not intend to be caught away from his post.

Thinking more of duty than danger, he popped his head over the parapet, and held it there just a moment too long. The German sniper, with his rifle set on our sentry post, pulled the trigger of his rifle. 'Crack', and poor Brady fell to the bottom of the trench, almost at the feet of the officer, who was just coming into the trench. We jumped to pick him up and we could see that he was badly wounded. He was shot clean through the head, blood was flowing from his nose and mouth and a great hole gaped in his skull. Quickly we did our best for him, the officer sending one of my men for the doctor. The doctor came quickly and did everything possible, but told us there was nothing else for it but to wait for the end. I couldn't keep my eyes from poor old Brady, lying there muttering, his head smothered in bloody bandages, his clothes covered in mud. A few hours later the end came as he muttered something about 'mother'.

That night we carried him a little behind the line and buried him. Poor Brady's death was a shock and a lesson to me, and I made up my mind that Fritz would have to be pretty sharp to catch me looking over the parapet long enough to sight a rifle on me.

During these four days Fritz shelled us with 5.9 guns. Down I would get to the bottom of the trench and almost try to burrow in like a rabbit, as the big shell came screaming down at us, the explosion making my trousers stick to my legs for a moment, and the feeling of relief as the shell burst a safe distance away, the pieces flying in all directions, humming their different tunes. Whether it was through God's will or Fritz's bad shooting that I am still living I don't know, but had one of those shells dropped on our trench it would certainly have been the end of us.

It was very cold, and we passed on the time bailing out the trench, chipping the sides, and keeping the firing step and parapet ready for instant use. At last the night of our relief came. The last few hours of waiting seeming like an eternity to me. Then dark figures began to creep up behind the trench and slide down to us. The usual handing over of trench stores took place, sentry posts were taken over, a little information about the enemy and his activities was given, and the scramble out of the trench began. Off again for the much-needed and very welcome rest in the village behind.

This night Fritz either saw or heard us being relieved. He turned a machine gun onto us and kept us lying low in the mud for at least ten minutes, bullets whistling just over our bodies. Eventually we made a dash for it, and after a lot of slipping, sliding and cursing we safely reached 'Smokers' Corner'. Here was cover at least from his rifle and machine-gun fire. We smoked and rested awhile, giving each section a chance to come up to us, and then our platoon officer called the roll and off we moved to the village.

On reaching the village our officer would bid us goodnight and we would disperse to our different billets, the villagers having waited up to greet us back again. The first thing to do after getting rid of our heavy equipment was to get off for rations and rum issue, the issue of rum this night usually being a little extra. Then we would settle down to a good supper and hot coffee and rum, at the same time eagerly opening and reading the letters from home.

During this period of rest I was moved from the estaminet into another and better billet, myself and three other men going into one house. We had the use of the front kitchen for ourselves, the civilians using the back kitchen and the bedrooms. The people in our new billet were very nice and did everything in their power to make us happy and comfortable. We were treated just like sons of the family, and during our subsequent periods of rest in the village they began to love us.

As we marched out of those horrible trenches, in the darkness of a winter's night, dirty and tired, they waited at their cottage doors, greeting each one of us by name, and offering up a prayer that each one of us was safely back again. Our beds would be made as comfy as possible, and meat, potatoes and vegetables would be steaming hot on the stove, ready to be served out along with the coffee and rum. The food, of course, was paid for before we had gone in the trenches. These good people were too poor to give much away. Should one of the boys be left behind in the trenches, never to see the village again, the grief of our hosts was painful to see. If told that one of the boys was wounded and on his way to Blighty, they were delighted and said 'Très bien'.

Sitting there round the kitchen stove in our stockinged feet, having discarded wet and muddy puttees and boots, we smoked and talked – mostly about war, we giving them our version of it and what our papers from home said about it, and they giving us the news from their newspapers. Then we retired to sleep our first real night's sleep for four days.

This four days in and four days out of the trenches carried on for some time. We had not really many casualties, there not being any real fighting, such as advances, at this time, both sides preferring to hold what they had, after Fritz's recent retreat from Paris, and of course this weather had also forced on to both sides this trench warfare. We had, of course, the usual exciting listening posts and patrols – to be sent out on listening post or patrol, lying in the mud in no-man's-land, on a December night, cold and hungry, staring through the darkness, straining one's ears, listening for any sound at all from the enemy that might convey something out of the ordinary, such as preparations for an attack, or working parties in no-man's-land, silently strengthening their defences; or lying stark still like a corpse, listening to an enemy patrol crawling about no-man's-land doing exactly the job that you have been sent out to do, rifles and bombs ready for instant use should either discover the other out there in the cold and mud, then back silently into the trench to report and to feel the horrible chill that sets in after lying perspiring in the cold mud on a December night, and a close proximity to death. If one was lucky a tot of rum would help to take away both the inward and outward feeling for a while. The horrible conditions in the trenches at that time were responsible for a lot of sickness.

Out in no-man's-land there lay the carcase of a dead cow, whose stench was almost unbearable when the wind was blowing in our direction. One night a couple of men were sent out with a can of petrol. Silently they made their way on hands and knees to the offensive carcase, and poured the petrol all over it, and returned safely to the trench. Then an officer fired off star lights into the air until he was lucky enough to drop a light on the dead cow. This good idea removed a serious nuisance out of no-man's-land, for which Fritz must also have been very thankful.

This was the kind of life we were living when Christmas Day of 1914 dawned. Our letters and parcels from home had come up during the night, along with the rations. We were also issued that Christmas morning with Christmas pudding and a little extra tot of rum. Opening our parcels, we shared the contents and prepared to make the day as merry as possible under the circumstances. Wishing each other a merry Christmas seemed such a farce, but nevertheless we did it and also joined together in singing carols.

Fritz across the way was also making merry, judging by the laughter and song that floated across no-man's-land to us. During the morning one of the Germans entertained us with German and English tunes on a cornet. The music echoed out across the open fields, the player being a credit to his band, and as he finished each item we clapped our hands and shouted across our applause and for encores. War certainly seemed forgotten for a while. Then about dinner time a flutter of excitement went down the trench. Coming across from the German trenches was a solitary German, carrying a white flag high above his head. Having come about half-way to our lines, he suddenly stopped and waited. Then one of our men was seen to go out and meet him, to bring him in to our lines. The German was the bearer of a message, asking our command for an armistice of two hours on this Christmas day, especially to bring in and bury a few dead bodies that still lay about in no-man's-land.

Unfortunately the German messenger who came over to our lines had not been blindfolded and led in by our man who went out to meet him, and consequently he had to be kept a prisoner of war. He protested and was awfully upset about it, but he had seen the position behind our lines, and that had to be kept from the enemy at all cost. Anyhow, over to the German lines went an English messenger, with a note that the armistice was agreed to and would be honoured. Then down the trench came the order to cease fire from such a time to such a time, two hours, and that no man must fire on any German seen in no-man's-land, during this armistice.

This was a great relief to us, and especially on such a morning, but we were all very cautious of putting our heads over the top for a while. First one and then another of the boys would venture to have a good look round, and we noticed also that Fritz seemed a little dubious. One or two of the most daring of the boys climbed out into no-man's-land and others soon followed suit, Fritz also feeling confident now that the armistice was genuine. Some of our boys tied up a sandbag and used it as a football, while a party of Germans enjoyed themselves sliding on a little frozen pond just in the rear of their trench. Both sides seemed to have no wish to get too far away from their trenches, seeming ready to spring back under cover should either side show the slightest sign of treachery.

Right across from our trench a party of Germans stood together, one of them waving what appeared to be a newspaper. We motioned them to bring it over to us, but Fritz would not have any. A corporal of ours said he would go over and fetch it. This seemed a risky thing to do, and although there was an armistice on at the time it required a nerve to walk across right up to Fritz's lines. But one or two of the boys dropped down into the trench and lay there with rifles ready, should Fritz be up to any dirty work.

On towards the German lines walked the corporal, beckoning the Germans to come out and meet him, but Fritz kept safely on the right side of his barbed wire. Once the corporal hesitated, but a cheery shout from the boys sent him on again. Right to the German barbed wire he went; the Germans greeted him with a cheer and clapped their hands, one of them leaning over the wire and handing him the German newspaper. Back came the corporal, walking like a good soldier and never looking behind him. None of us could read German so the paper was not any source of information to us.

Some of the boys made good use of the armistice to improve the comfort of the trench. They gathered wood and brought straw from an old barn close by. Then came the order for every man to get back into his trench. The armistice was over. Perhaps it was way back at headquarters, but those two hours that Christmas day had been very sweet to Tommy and Fritz. To get from between those two walls of clay and stretch one's cramped and aching limbs and look over the landscape without the fear of a bullet in one's head was too glorious to be wiped out with one quick military order, and the boys were reluctant to start fighting again.

We also noticed that Fritz was feeling likewise. The German command were also having difficulty in getting Fritz back into the trenches. Hours went by and still men were walking about on the parapet. Right opposite us, Fritz stuck up a broom handle in the trench with a white handkerchief pinned to it. Not a shot was fired from either side. Messages came along the trenches threatening drastic measures if men didn't cease walking about on top, and still peace reigned in no-man's-land.

41

Fritz shouted across 'No shoot' and similar things in French, and the boys answered back in the same strain. Then a machine gun of ours burst out and a battery of artillery thundered out in the rear. An officer here and there fired his revolver over at Fritz. The comfortably housed and well fed 'Heads' in the rear had done their duty. They had started the war again. Then a few days afterwards when we got our letters and papers from home we read of the British public's horror at their troops actually fraternising with the horrible German troops. Even the clergy had condemned us for such un-British conduct. Condemned, for conduct that gave us a few hours' respite from the awful job of murder. Conduct that was brought about because it was Christmas Day, the day of 'good will to all men', at a time and place where men could really show the true spirit of Christmas.[6]

We had dared to stop the bloody game of war a few hours longer than the 'official' period. Men who were half starved, dirty, lousy, suffering unbelievable mental and physical tortures, for a purpose that not one in a hundred of them could definitely state – can one imagine the feelings of these men at this ingratitude from their own country? No wonder that the common and general wish of these men was that those well fed and comfortable critics were in the trenches opposite, in the place of a more friendly enemy.

During the four days which included Christmas, the weather was fairly bad and it froze hard on the last day of the four. During the day I had had a nap of about two hours. While sleeping, my feet, which I had curled up under me, had dropped down in the bottom of the trench in which was a few inches of water. It was freezing hard at the time and when I awoke I had to break the ice which had formed round my ankles to get my feet out of the water. I did not feel much effect from the freezing except a kind of numbness in my feet.

That night the Royal Lancs came again to relieve us. The usual hand-over, and out we scrambled once again, to make our way back to Le Bizet and another much-needed four-day rest. After the usual slipping and sliding across the open fields, I reached the hard road, and then I noticed that my feet felt rather queer, as if I had got soft pads under my boots. However, I did not worry much and carried on to the village, but – bad luck for me – I was detailed for billet guard that night.

The three men who made up the guard that I was in charge of were billeted a little higher up the street, so I carted my bed and blankets up to their billet and settled down for the remainder of the night; being corporal of the guard, I had to settle down fully dressed. The sentries relieved one another and called me when it was daylight. When the last sentry did waken me, I found that my feet were horribly swollen. I could not stand up on them, and the boys had to cut my boots to get them off my feet. The old lady in the billet got the boys to carry me into the kitchen and place me near the stove. She made me hot coffee and did everything she could for me.

Then, at time for sick parade, one of the boys carried me on his back round to the doctor. He told me that I had got frozen feet, and sent me off to a temporary hospital in the village. During the day Fritz shelled the village and put a shell right into the hospital. Luckily at the time I was in the opposite end of the building to that which was struck with the shell and did not catch any harm. I was only in this place one night, and next morning I was put into a horse ambulance and taken to Nieppe, a village a little further down the line. Here again I was examined and stayed one night, which was New Year's Eve of 1915. On New Year's Day I was put on a motor ambulance and taken to Hazebrouck. Here I was examined again and labelled, that is, a label was fastened to my tunic buttonhole, giving my number, name, regiment and complaint, and then I was put on an ambulance train. Now I knew that I was going right down the line, but where to I had no idea.

That night of the first day of the year of 1915, the train moved off. There were four beds in my compartment, fixed as the seats and luggage racks are in an ordinary corridor coach. Each bed was occupied; three other boys lying there with bullet and shell wounds, and myself with two dead feet. We were very comfortable and smoked and talked of our different regiments and fronts. The nurse came along, bringing cups of hot cocoa and sandwiches.

Outside, as the train sped along through the darkness, it rained and snowed, sleet beat on the carriage windows and as I listened to it I thought of the boys I had left back in Le Bizet. They were due back again to the trenches that night, and I knew that at that moment they would be plodding on through the sleet and the mud. I could plainly see their swaying figures, ducking and dodging in the glare of a star light, glistening in the raindrops, and hear the curses and muttered oaths as they stepped into a flooded shell-hole, to struggle on its slippery sides until the next man gave a helping hand.

I was a casualty with two dead feet, but how sorry I felt for those fit men as I lay in that cosy train, every minute taking me one more mile from those horrible trenches. During the journey we learned from the nurse that our destination was Boulogne. I had a good sleep in the train and was awakened by the nurse, who told me to prepare to be moved. I noticed RAMC men dashing along the corridors with stretchers, and soon they appeared in my compartment. I was transferred to a stretcher and carried out of the train, and as the bearers stepped on to the platform my heart missed a beat. There, right alongside of us, was a big hospital ship. For a moment I thought I was going on that ship and right away to England, but it was not to be. They slid me into a motor ambulance and away up on to the cliffs to hospital. Here I was soon put to bed, my feet bathed and powdered, and a hot meal served to me.

This hospital had been a hotel, I believe, and made into a hospital for the Canadians. Anyhow, the room I was in appeared to be an ordinary bedroom; there were four cots in it, the other three beds being occupied with men with frozen feet like myself. We were treated very nicely here and we had no complaints. The treatment consisted mainly of bathing and powdering our feet. We lay in bed with our feet propped up and exposed outside the bedclothes.

The doctor would come round daily and, standing at the foot of our bed, he would ask us how we felt, at the same time pushing a needle gently into our feet. This method told him when life was coming back to our feet, as we naturally gave a jump on feeling the prick of the needle. Of course we could get out of bed and sit on chairs round the fire in our room, but to let the heat of the fire get to our feet meant awful pain, so instead of sitting the ordinary way in front of a fire we had to sit so that our feet were farthest from it. We also went along the corridor to the lavatory without help, doing this on all fours, hands and knees, the nurses having a good laugh as some of the boys went along barking like a dog. Then there was the struggle to get on to the WC without touching anything with one's toes. Many a contortionist would have been jealous to see us perform this trick. But, putting all joking at one side, to have caught anything with one's feet was awful pain.

Again I was one of the lucky ones. In the next room to ours was a boy who had to lose both his feet to save his life. When I got walking about fairly nicely I went in to see him. He was quite aware that he was going to lose his feet, but he was quite cheerful, and said, 'Never mind, I have finished going into those —— trenches.'

After about nine days I was marked out to convalescence, and along with a few more boys I left the hospital to make room for others, and toddled down beside the river to what appeared to be an old factory with the works taken out. This was just a place to rest for a while, until our feet got something like normal. There were a couple of stoves in the place and we had the trestle, straw palliasse beds and army rations. There was one parade a day, at ten o'clock each morning, which was a 'go as you please' walk of about two miles, and if one preferred to remain in bed it was quite all right.

All the cash I had in my pockets on leaving hospital was one franc, and no prospects of getting any more for some time. We did manage to get an issue or two of cigarettes at the factory, through the generosity of the officer in charge.

That evening I decided to have a walk out before retiring. I knew nothing about Boulogne and could only speak a word or two of French, but I set off, taking notice of churches and prominent buildings so as to be able to trace my way back. I looked at the estaminets and cafés and could have worried a good supper, but I somehow didn't like the idea of parting with my last franc. At last I decided that I had walked far enough on my poor feet and turned my face towards the factory again. In turning suddenly I bumped into two young ladies, knocking one of them down. I hastily helped her on to her feet again and apologised, in English of course. They answered something in French, but they may as well have held their breath as utter any French to me. They evidently knew nothing of English and then they seemed to be tickled by the comical situation and had a good laugh.

I was in no particular hurry and had a laugh too. Here I thought was going to be a little entertainment and fun. They talked to each other and laughingly tried to ask me something. After a lot of talking and gesticulating, which we all enjoyed so much, we kind of got introduced. They knew the factory where I was staying and kindly escorted me there. Of course, I had to promise to meet them again, and the making of arrangements to meet again the following evening was another ten minutes' good fun. After a lot of finger counting and stamping of feet and the help of a nearby church clock, I bid my friends 'bonsoir' with the knowledge that I had to be at that same spot again the following evening at five thirty.

During my stay at the factory I dined more at my friends' house and spent more time in their company than at the factory. They kept me going in cigarettes and anything else I wanted, and considerably helped to improve my French.

Alas, all good times must come to an end some time, and my name appeared on the list to return to unit. I was once more fixed up as a fighting man. My friends came to the railway sidings to see me off, bringing with them a huge packet of sandwiches and stuffing into my pockets a box of cigarettes and a ten-franc note to help me on my way. Into the cattle-trucks we climbed, and, with my friends shouting their best wishes, we moved off on another of those long uncomfortable journeys up the line. I was not feeling too happy, knowing what was in front of me, but I settled down as cosy as possible, smoking and day-dreaming while the old truck jolted along. After the cold and painful ride, a good stiff march brought me to Le Bizet once again.

Fortunately for me, the old battalion was out resting. I rejoined my old company and soon learned who had been killed and wounded during my absence. I could see that the village had been knocked about a lot by Fritz's shell fire, and the boys told me that Fritz was making things hot nowadays up in the trenches. I soon realised how true this was, the Germans shelling us heavily each day and continually sniping, causing the battalion quite a lot of casualties.

Running through our front line and right on through the German's front line was a country road. On one side of this road, and in no-man's-land was a row of cottages. These cottages were in excellent order and still contained the furniture and cooking utensils, etc., that they contained when the tenants left them hurriedly before the swift German advance. The fact that they were in no-man's-land had saved them from the artillery fire, but during the night time these cottages were the scene of some desperate fighting, as the patrols of both sides sought to gain possession of them.

Our commander decided that these cottages must be taken and held by our company. So over we went in good strength, took possession of the cottages and by morning, with jolly hard work, we had sandbagged and barricaded the end nearest to the Germans, also knocking a way right through the whole row as a communication to our front line.

Only ten yards away from our barricaded wall commenced another row of cottages, barricaded and held by Germans. Through our loopholes and over the back yard wall we could plainly hear Fritz talking. Although so terribly near to the enemy, we were quite comfortable, making a fire in the grate and cooking our meals and lying on the beds, just like being at home. The cellars still contained potatoes and turnips, which we certainly helped ourselves to. The boys would shout over to Fritz and Fritz would answer back in English, one of them arguing that he knew Manchester as well as any of us.

One day we were sitting round the fire in the kitchen watching a lovely stew bubble in a great pan, our mouths watering in anticipation of a good dinner, when a few quick rifle shots rang out. There was a dull rumbling sound in the kitchen chimney and down came a couple of bricks, bringing with them clouds of soot and dust, knocking the pan clean off the fire and scattering the stew and soot all over the floor. We soon realised what had happened, and out into the back yard dashed the boys to the barricade, for quite a time the air was thick with curses and horrible wishes being sent over to Fritz. Loud laughter from the Germans told us how pleased they were with the success of their shots.

Sometimes as we walked about the back yard behind the barricade small bombs came whistling down out of the air. We were puzzled at these bombs, and if a man was unlucky enough to be near one when it exploded he received twenty of thirty small wounds. Headquarters issued an order that the first of these bombs which failed to explode was to be sent down to them. We found out in this way that they were a rifle grenade, that is, a small bomb fired into the air from a rifle, which meant that they could be sent much farther than the ordinary jam-tin bomb which we were using.[7]

Carefully peeping through a bedroom window our sentries could see well into the German lines, and one of our officers used to shoot through a hole in the roof each day, sniping Germans who were working in a school yard some five or six hundred yards away, marking down and keeping careful count of his hits on a rafter. One night Pte —— was on sentry duty at this bedroom window. It was quite easy to sit on the bed and keep a look-out towards Fritz's barricade built across the road, but such a cosy post was too much for Pte ——. He was caught lying fast asleep on the bed by the patrolling officer, who warned him of the serious consequences of such conduct on active service, but later in the night the officer again caught him fast asleep and this time reported him.

Poor old ——, a jolly good soldier, as strong as an elephant, always willing to carry a weaker comrade's pack besides his own, was tried by court martial, found guilty, and shot at dawn. The crime and the punishment were read out to us as a lesson to all who might neglect duty, but it was not the lesson it was intended to be; it just fanned the flame of hatred against the men who did their fighting in big châteaux and their marching in motor cars.

Both sides had been mining extensively in the Le Touquet area. Part of the Le Touquet defences known as Railway Fort had been encircled by an underground ring to prevent the Germans from sapping beneath it, and galleries were also dug under the German lines. On the night of 7–8 April 1915 a German counter-mine was discovered, and at 8.30 on the morning of 9 April British sappers blew it up. German casualties were heavy, and the Germans responded by shelling Le Touquet fiercely.

During our occupation of these cottages, Fritz was busy mining right under them, and as we lay on the floor we could hear the dull sounds as the German engineers dug away beneath us, never knowing the moment he might decide to blow us all to eternity. At the same time our engineers were digging away under the Germans' house and barricade. It seemed to become quite a race who would complete the job first. The thought of being blown sky high got on our nerves, and it was a great relief when one night our engineers brought with them lots of gun cotton, carrying it down into the mine and packing it ready for firing.

Wires were connected to the mine and just before dawn we received orders to evacuate the cottages and fall back into the front-line trench. As dawn came we got orders to fire rapidly; the rapid firing went on for twenty minutes or so. Fritz naturally thought we were preparing to attack and rushed up reserves into his front line. This was just what we wanted: the mine would certainly have a great deal more effect.

The order came along to cease fire, with a second order for every man to keep well under cover. A minute later the ground shook and the trench seemed to rock, and with a muffled roar a blue flame shot up into the sky. Showers of bricks and dirt came hurtling over to our trench and one or two men were hurt. Pieces of cloth floated down through the clouds of dust; whether it was sandbags or uniforms I don't know – probably both. Then a swift order came for us to reoccupy the cottages again, and as we dashed to the end barricade in the back yard we saw that one German had been blown clean onto an outhouse. Right under our noses, within ten yards of our rifle barrels, another German calmly placed a ladder against the outhouse, climbed it and, lifting his wounded comrade on to his shoulder, carried him to safety. We were too taken aback at such bravery to shoot and, as our officer said, he was too brave to die. He had most certainly earned the Iron Cross.

Later on Fritz withdrew his men from the front line while he heavily shelled our cottages, forcing us to abandon them and fall back into the front-line trench, the cottages again becoming the nest of night patrols.

This four days in and four days out of the line carried on until April, and by this time Fritz had made a mess of our rest village and also of the battalion. Most of the civilians had fled from Le Bizet for their lives, and others had been ordered to go for their own safety by the army authorities.

However, we were to have a rest and another brigade came up to relieve us, our battalion moving into billets in Armentières, about another four miles behind the lines. Armentières at this time had hardly been touched by the war, life going on almost normally in the town – just a little excitement when a German plane appeared overhead and, quickly dropping his bombs on the town, hurriedly retreated over the German lines. Here we had long hours of parade and were kept busy cleaning and polishing equipment and uniforms.

We were allowed out in the town in the evening and the boys were out to have the best possible time. Drink flowed freely in the estaminets and cafés, and as the music and singing went on the boys danced with mademoiselles in the flimsiest of dresses, or flirted with them at the tables, using the most vulgar expressions. All the evening Tommies could be seen either going to or coming from the girls' rooms upstairs, queues actually forming on the stairs leading to these rooms.

During one of these riotous nights, when the queue of drink-sodden Tommies almost reached from the first girl's room to the floor below, a sudden command of 'Attention' rang out. As the boys did their best to stand upright, into the estaminet walked the battalion padre along with the sergeant of the military police.[8] The padre glared at the queue on the stairs and then at the tables swimming in cognac and *vin blanc*. Then in scathing words he started to address us. He told us that the conditions under which we had lived for the last few months were no excuse for our beastly conduct. He asked us if we had forgotten that we were Englishmen, or forgotten our mothers and sisters and wives, or had no shame at all. During all this the queue on the stairs had disappeared; men left their drink and slunk out into the street, but the padre had promised to report to the commanding officer.

He certainly kept his word, for the next day the battalion was formed up on parade to be lectured by the colonel. Angrily our commander rode onto parade, and away he blazed about our conduct the night before in the Rue des Bons Enfants, as reported to him by the padre. 'The irony of it!' he said. 'Do you know what "Rue des Bons Enfants" means? It means "The street of good children".' A low titter went round the battalion, but the colonel, fire flying from his eyes, his horse restless under his anger, said he would put a stop to such conduct, and bawled out orders that the troops would only be allowed out for two hours in the evening and that only with passes, which would be issued to 25 per cent of the battalion at a time. Anyhow, the whole rest only lasted a fortnight and then we began to pack up for another move.

We did enjoy one luxury while staying at Armentières. One morning our platoon was told to fall in with towels. Off we marched to a village a couple of miles away, turning into the yard of what looked like an old brewery. In the open air we stripped off every stitch of clothing, tied them in a bundle with a piece of string and attached a label to them on which was written our regimental number. Then we dashed in the old building in our birthday suits. Inside were two great big wine vats, half filled with fairly hot water. Into these we had to climb, about 15 men to a vat. Pieces of blue mottled soap were given to us, and middle-aged men and youths jostled and splashed about in the tightly packed vat, doing our best to scrub each other's backs and bend down to wash our legs. We had a good bit of fun and one can imagine the remarks and rude jokes made by the men. We thoroughly enjoyed the soaking our lice-ridden bodies were getting, and our officer made sure that every man stayed in the vat until the order to get out was given. We rubbed ourselves down with our towels and dashed outside for our clothes.

We found them where we had left them in a bundle on the floor; a cloud of steam was rising from them and they were quite hot to the touch. It appeared that while we were bathing our clothes had been put into a pressurised steam cylinder and fumigated. A clean shirt and socks were thrown to us and we got dressed. Our clothes were still warm and terribly creased. We looked more like old tramps than soldiers. Yes, the fumigation had killed the lice all right and we had some relief from the itching and scratching, but the seams of our pants and coats still held thousands of lice eggs and we soon discovered that the warmth of our bodies hatched them out again. Soon we were scratching ourselves sore once more and doing our best to rid ourselves of these tormenting creatures.

On a sunny day we would fix bayonets to our rifles, not to stab the things but to stick the bayonet into the ground and stand the rifle up with the butt in the air. Soon the hot sun would draw the lice from the seams of the shirt, hanging on the butt of the rifle, out on top in a squirming bunch. The flame of a match soon despatched that lot, then the flame was run along the seams of the shirt, and one could hear the crackle of frying lice eggs as the heat destroyed them.

I found out that there were more pests like Germans and lice to kill in trench warfare. I don't remember where or when this incident happened but I think it is worth mentioning. It was a very nice summer's day and we were resting out of the front line. A circular canvas compound was erected, about 15 feet in diameter and 4 feet 6 inches high, quite close to our tent. The men were ordered to go in the circle and take with them their shaving kit, then to strip off and shave their private parts thoroughly. If men could not do this awkward job themselves, then they had to shave each other. During this operation one can imagine the remarks made by the men. It was a bloody, painful, and still humorous performance, especially using a blunt army razor.

After shaving, we were given lots of a dark blue ointment which we plastered all over our lower parts. The boys called the ointment 'blue unction', which we had to abide with for 3 or 4 days before washing it off. We were supposed to have a bad dose of 'crabs'. I don't know what the medical name is. They were a tiny crab-like creature that attacked the lower parts of the abdomen and lived under the skin, so that if you happened to have these irritating little creatures they were very hard to get rid of. I think the shaving and blue unction did the trick. There was no further 'Operation Crab'.

3

Gassed

On 22 April 1915 the Germans attacked French troops north of Ypres, near the point where French and British lines joined, behind a cloud of chlorine gas. This, the first use of gas on the Western Front, caused widespread consternation amongst the French units concerned, many of them North Arican, and a four-mile gap was torn in the Allied lines. The initial attack was followed by further German assaults and numerous British counter-attacks in an effort to regain the lost ground. On 1 May the British withdrew to a new line closer to Ypres. This had been recommended by Sir Horace Smith-Dorrien, commander of the British Second Army, who had a history of bad relations with the British commander-in-chief, Sir John French, but Smith-Dorrien was relieved of his command and the withdrawal was carried out by Sir Herbert Plumer. Many historians have suggested that a large-scale retirement to a line west of Ypres would have been preferable. However, the psychological motives for retaining Ypres, whose salient had already cost thousands of British lives, and which was the only major Belgian town still in Allied hands, were considerable.

The battle – known as the Second Battle of Ypres – drew in British troops from other sectors, amongst them the 2nd Lancashire Fusiliers, which left its billets in the 'Blue Factory' at Nieppe on 27 April. It marched by way of Bailleul to Vlamertinghe, and on the evening of the 29th it moved up into the line, past what the regimental history called 'an ever-increasing number of retreating and panic-stricken French native troops . . . and the numerous evidences, patent to eye and nose, of the effects of gas on men, animals and vegetation'.

We marched off again from Armentières and came to a halt at Bailleul. Here we rested for the night. The battalion split up in barns and houses, or any old place that had a few timbers that could be called a roof. Rumour was flying about that we were on our way to Ypres, and next morning we moved off again, certainly in the direction of Ypres.

After a gruelling march of over twenty miles we came to a halt in a field. The thunder of the guns was quite loud now, and big shells were dropping not far away, some going right overhead to drop miles in rear of us. Tea was made in the field kitchens and rations issued to us. While having tea we were warned to be prepared for the trenches that night. This was very cheerful news after a march of over twenty miles. We were also warned that it was a 'hot shop' and we already knew by the sound of the guns that there was plenty of iron flying about.

Also about this time, Fritz was beginning to use his infernal poison gas and we were told to expect it coming over any time the wind was favourable. Each section commander was issued with flannelette and elastic, and a sample 'gas protector', which consisted of the flannelette folded two or three times thick, to be placed over the mouth and nose and held in position with a piece of elastic round the head. We were told to make ourselves one of these protectors at the first opportunity. We laughed at the idea of poison gas and stuffed the flannelette away at the bottom of our packs, little dreaming how soon we should need it.

After tea we moved off up the line, guides having come down from the front line to show us our way in the trenches. By the time we had gone a couple of miles it was quite dark, and Fritz was sending over shells pretty merrily, spraying the road with shrapnel and wounding a few men. Our commanding officer in the lead was also slightly wounded, and the second in command took charge.[9]

On we marched, the flash of the guns and the bursting shells almost lighting up the way, the buildings on either side of the road without roofs and windows, looking gaunt and stark. Here and there we had to make a detour in the road, round a pile of bricks and mortar, where a big shell had made a fair hit and razed a whole building to the ground. Then in front of us was the Ypres canal which we had to cross on a pontoon bridge. This bridge was a proper death trap. Fritz kept up a hot fire on it, sending over a salvo of shells at once, with only a few seconds of grace between each batch. Over this bridge the battalion went, a few men at a time, between the salvos of shells. We had to run for our lives across the bridge, darting for cover immediately on the other side, and as we ran over the swaying bridge the shells were screaming on their way towards us. At the same time, bumping and lurching across the crazy bridge were the gun limbers, the horses galloping madly on as if they knew the terrible danger they were in, the limber drivers shouting the horses on still faster and faster.

On we went, following our guides, the roar of guns and bursting shells drowning most other noises. Then down we dropped into a communication trench, heaving a sigh as we felt the shelter of its walls. After seeming to walk on duckboards and round turns for miles we came to the reserve trenches. These trenches were held by Indian soldiers, the Gurkhas, who were cowering down as far as possible in the bottom of the trench, terrified of the big shells Fritz was sending over.

After wandering about in the trenches apparently lost and almost exhausted, we got settled in a rather shallow trench.[10] We had relieved the PPCLI, or Princess Patricia's Canadian Light Infantry. Our trench was a second line about fifty yards behind the front line. Very soon the men who were not told off for sentry duty were down and fast asleep. It had been a strenuous day and feet and shoulders were aching with marching and carrying the fighting kit of an infantryman.

Morning came and we were able to take stock of our surroundings. Our trench was on a rise and looking right along to the left we could see a section of the front line held by the Gurkhas, and in front of them a ridge and a farmhouse held by the Germans. That same afternoon we saw the Gurkhas go over the top in an attempt to take the ridge, but Fritz's withering fire mowed them down and the gallant Gurkhas fell back to their own lines.[11] We realised what was in store for us, should we get the order to go over.

A little distance behind our trench was an old barn, or what was left of one, but behind its battered walls were dozens of dead bodies waiting to be buried.[12] Fritz seemed to have known this and sent over a few incendiary shells, setting the old barn on fire, and as it lit up the surrounding country the stench of burning flesh floated over the trenches. Inside the barn were also a few spare boxes of ammunition. These were banging off all night, and the light and flying bullets made it very dangerous to knock about outside the trench.

The second day in the trenches was a lovely day. It was warm and bright and a slight breeze was blowing over from the German lines. It was about tea time and the day had been fairly quiet. The guns had been much quieter. We sat in our trench looking over towards the ridge on our left that Fritz held. Then we noticed a thick smoke coming out of Fritz's front line and blowing over to the English lines. It seemed strange for Fritz to have a fire on so fine an afternoon and give so lovely a mark to our artillery.[13]

Then we noticed a greenish yellow fog also blowing across towards us, and it seemed to dawn on all of us at once that Fritz was sending over his infernal gas. Immediately there was a shout of 'Gas' and a wild rush for flannelette and water, but before we could get these and put them to our mouths the horrible gas was on us. Only God knows my own feelings as I got the first taste of it. I had no knowledge how soon it killed, and for a moment I thought my end had come. Some of the boys soaked their handkerchiefs in water and held them to their mouths and noses.

With muffled orders and signs our officer got us to stand to, our rifles with fixed bayonets in one hand and the primitive gas mask held to our mouths with the other, waiting for Fritz to come over after his gas had done its work. My throat and chest seemed to be burning out and I could not stop coughing. Some of the boys could stick it no longer and began to climb out of the trench, to be sent back to their position with the officer's revolver at their heads. The din now was terrific; Fritz was sending over shells for all he was worth and raking our trenches with machine guns and our batteries, expecting an attack to follow behind the gas, were firing rapidly onto the German lines.

In a few minutes that lovely afternoon had been transformed into a scene of hell. The air was thick with shrapnel and screaming shells and bullets whistled just over our heads. Men spat and coughed and cursed

Fritz and his terrible gas, as they bent low for safety from the flying shells and tried to get away from the poisonous gas. Suddenly there was a noise of thundering feet on top of our trench and figures began to jump clean over our trench and heads. They were our men from the front line, and as this went on someone passed the word along the trench to retire. Whether this order was official or not I don't know, but there was a rush to get out of the trench; our officer tried to calm the men, but he might as well have tried to calm a rough sea. Away we ran across the open, not knowing or caring where to, so long as it was further away from that horrible gas and bombardment.

Big shells screamed over us and shrapnel burst amongst us, their deadly contents pit-patting into the earth around us; bullets hissed past us, mixed with shouts and curses as some unfortunate fellow was struck down. Sound men helped wounded pals along, or left them when it was plain to see that they would fight no more. On we struggled, our chests bursting and throats choked up with a greenish froth, which oozed out of our mouths and down on to our tunics, as it does on a horse that has had a long, mad gallop. One gallant young officer did his best to stem the tide, ordering first one and then another, at the point of a revolver, to halt and man a nearby shell-hole. His bravery did not last long. A huge shell literally blew him to pieces.

We passed the French batteries of famous 75s, the gunners in their shirt-sleeves loading for all they were worth, the officer in charge, with drawn sword, running from one gun to another, and when he saw they were loaded and ready shouting at the top of his voice, 'Allez!'. As the guns spat out and the earth flew up from the German front line, he danced around with delight.

While we were near this battery Fritz sent over a nasty shrapnel shell. We heard it coming, right for us, and dropped quickly to the floor. It burst with terrific force right on top of us. I felt a sharp smack and burn on the back of my neck and yelled out with pain, also hearing one of my pals give a horrible groan. Poor fellow, he was killed instantly with a nose-cap right through his back, while the piece that hit me had only torn through my tunic collar and broken the skin.

After the French gunners had promised to see to our dead comrade and a bandage had been put on my neck, we moved on. We were in the streets of Ypres now and broken limbers, carts, burnt lorries and dead horses were lying about the place.

Suddenly, out of a battered house came a sergeant of the Royal Engineers, dragging with him a man in civilian clothes. No sooner were they in the street than the engineer drew a revolver and shot the civilian dead, explaining to us a moment afterwards that he had caught the civilian telephoning to the enemy from the cellar of the house. Leaving the man lying where he was shot, the engineer went back into the house to cut the wires and destroy the phone.

Some Belgian soldiers, noticing our plight, took us into a billet of theirs and gave us some salt and water to drink to make us sick, and in that way vomit up the green slime that was almost choking us, but we could not get the salt and water down, and after a rest we pushed on, just three of us together now. On we struggled, still wearing most of our equipment and carrying our rifles, but at last we could carry them no further and dropped them by the side of the road.

We had passed a battalion of soldiers going up to re-man our vacant trenches, vacant with the exception of one man, a man on whose chest was the ribbon of the DCM. This man, a machine gunner, had remained behind with his gun and as Fritz had come over behind his gas Jack Lynn, which was the name of this brave man, had mown them down, holding our trenches alone, firing away at the enemy, almost choked and blinded with the horrible gas. The soldiers who re-manned our trenches found him there, still holding the enemy back and gasping for breath. Two days afterwards poor Jack died from the effects of gas. He was awarded the VC, and he certainly earned it.[14]

We were miles away from the trenches now and beginning to feel exhausted, and a little further on one of the three dropped down and could go no further. While we lay there exhausted, an officer came along on horseback and, noticing our plight, he asked us what was the matter and where we belonged. Having got this information, he sent the orderly who was riding with him back for an ambulance. This was soon on the spot and away we sped to a dressing station. Here men were lying all over the place, wounded and gassed. Some lay dead, having succumbed to their terrible wounds or the gas. We were put down on some straw to wait our turn for attention, but the doctor and orderlies were quite puzzled as to how to treat us.

After lying there an hour or two, during which time we were offered tea and food, neither of which we wanted, we were again placed into ambulances and taken further down the line to Bailleul. The worst part of this gas business was that we could not be drawing at the old fag; smoking was out of the question, and if only the smoke from some fellow passing us reached our nostrils, it just smelt and tasted like Fritz's gas.

At Bailleul they put us into a school, used as a hospital, where we only stayed the night. The next morning we had to fall in and again be examined. By now I seemed to have got over the worst of the gas and was feeling much better, and fully expected the doctor to make me fit for duty again, and to be sent back up the line. But to my great surprise and delight I was labelled for hospital down the line.

That afternoon saw us comfortably settled down in an ambulance train, and after a long ride we arrived at Rouen, motor ambulances meeting the train here and quickly transferring us to No. 12 General Hospital, where I was put to bed in the same hut as about a score more gas cases. Although feeling all right, I was given nothing but milk and medicine to drink, and a cup to spit in. It was quite plain to me that the cure was going to be starvation.

In a few days' time I was quite ill and too weak to sit up in bed, and I began to think that the gas was just beginning to do its dirty work. I certainly felt that my end was coming, the bed was saturated in perspiration from my weak body.

While I was lying here some great professor from London, Professor Haldane I believe it was, came to visit us and study our case. He asked quite a lot of questions and spent quite a long time at our bedsides, and then he said quite openly beside my bed that for men under forty there was every chance, but he had not such hopes for men over forty years of age.[15]

Then one morning the nurse asked me if I would like a little breakfast. I managed to eat half a slice of bread and butter, and then round came the doctor on his daily visit. Sitting on my bed, he smiled and asked me if I was feeling fit to travel. I stared at him and said, 'It all depends where to, Sir.' He smiled again and said, 'Well, we'll see tomorrow when you have had a little more food.' The following morning came and the doctor again asked me if I was fit to travel, and I said, 'If it is to Blighty, Sir, I can walk it.' 'All right,' he said, 'you shall go to Blightly tomorrow.' The next day two orderlies placed a stretcher alongside my bed. The nurse put me some clean pyjamas on and then the orderlies placed me gently on the stretcher and carried me out to a waiting motor ambulance, which sped away down to the docks, where, lashed to the quay, lay a hospital ship.

I was quickly and gently transferred to the ship and made very comfortable in a bunk down below. A nurse came along bringing me food and drink and asking if I felt all right. I said yes, but shortly afterwards I went awfully queer. An orderly brought the doctor to me and he told the nurse to have me removed up on deck. I was carried on deck and placed as comfy as possible on two deck chairs, and I felt much better in the fresh air than in the stuffy bunk down below.

During the evening we set sail for England. Propped up in my deck chairs I could look out over the wake of the ship, and staring through the darkness I noticed a red light that seemed to be following us all the way. Owing to my weak state, my nerves were on edge and I imagined the red light to be a submarine about to torpedo us and I was getting quite worked up and alarmed. An officer of the ship came and sat down beside me, and quickly I drew his attention to the red light and told him that it had been following us for hours. He said, 'Yes, my boy, we want that red light to follow us, it is our escort.' Of course, I felt much easier, then soon I must have fallen off to sleep.

I was awakened by a couple of orderlies who told me that we had arrived at Southampton and that they were going to carry me down to the ambulance train. In a few minutes time I was lying quite comfortably in the train, and the thought that I was once more safe in old England, and only a train journey from home, made me feel much better. The next thing I knew, we were being whirled away to Birmingham. People cheered us and waved as we sped along, and in a few hours we drew into Birmingham station. Private cars waited to convey us to the hospital, the cars being driven by their owners, and in the cars were stocks of cigarettes, chocolates and fruit for our benefit. As we sped along the roads people cheered and cheered, and crowds assembled outside Dudley Road Infirmary, which was my destination, to see us carried from the cars, saying a cheery word to us or slipping a gift of some sort onto our stretchers.

Inside the infirmary we were very soon made comfortable, but I got a shock and felt quite mad when the nurse came round and asked me if I would like a cup of milk, as we had arrived sooner than expected, and tea wasn't ready. No wonder my answer was rather rude, after living on nothing but milk for eight days. Anyhow, feeling much better after tea, I apologised to the nurse and explained to her what my diet had been in France, and that the mere mention of milk made my blood boil.

I was in this hospital for twelve days, and at the end of that time I was very pleased to be marked out for convalescence. I was fed up staring round the ward at other sick cases, and the food was certainly not of the best or of large quantity. I was truly disappointed, and other boys in my ward were also asking to be marked fit for convalescence. Along with a few other boys in the infirmary I received vouchers and reports to proceed to Summerdown Camp at Eastbourne. This was a lovely camp about a mile outside the town and at the foot of the slopes of Beachy Head. Here we had comfortable beds in army huts and plenty of good food, practically no parading to do and the whole time to ourselves.

All kinds of sport were indulged in and we were allowed out into the town from one o'clock until one wished to return, providing of course that on coming in you slipped over the wire fence round the camp and not through the gate and past the guard on duty there. We went bathing in the sea and crabbing on the rocks below the promenade, or we took out a rowing boat, for which we were charged only half the usual price, and spent a couple of hours rowing around, often leaving the boat a mile or so away from the place we had loaned it, causing the old boatmen hours of work gathering in the lost boats. While here we wore the old familiar blue hospital suits and red ties, with the usual 'Bond Street cut', half a yard turned up at the legs of the trousers and five or six inches of a turn-up at the sleeves. Anyhow, the boys at the camp soon improved their appearance by having the suits made fit better and buying new ties and fancy socks, etc.

Sweethearts and wives came over and got digs in the town, and almost daily came up to the camp, spending hours inspecting our living quarters and often staying to dine with their husbands and boys. Around our huts were lovely gardens, there being quite a competition for the most lovely hut and garden. Inside the huts we did our own decorations, painting all kinds of pictures on the asbestos lining of our hut around our beds.

We could strike off from the rear of our camp and climb on to the top of Beachy Head, there to lie down and look right out over the channel to France, or sit up there in the evening having tea and watching those small airships of ours patrolling the channel, on the look-out for U-boats. The well-to-do people around Eastbourne would send their cars and chauffeurs up to the camp to take us for lovely rides out to Pevensey and Hastings, the cars always loaded with cigarettes, fruit and sweets. Very often the owners would come up themselves and after our spin round they would take us to their places for tea, often finishing the evening off with a theatre or music-hall visit.

One day, one of the grandest hotels on the front sent up to the camp an invitation to 100 of the boys to luncheon. The wealthy guests at the hotel drove up in their own cars to the camp to fetch us. On arrival at the hotel the proprietor received each one of us personally, and we were directed to our tables in a gorgeously decorated dining-room by some wealthy or titled person staying at the hotel. The tables were full of food and dainties of every kind. Not a servant of the hotel was to be seen. The titled and wealthy guests had become our servants for at least an hour or two. Lady Paget was the waiter at my table, and tears streamed down her cheeks as she fed one of our boys who had both arms in slings.[16]

During the meal we stopped for a moment to listen to a speech by the proprietor of the hotel. It was a speech I shall never forget – one that made me feel proud that I had fought, and one that filled my throat to bursting point. 'Eat and drink,' he said; 'it is what you are entitled to. It is what you have well and truly earned. Today I, and these great people, are your servants. We owe you a lot. Don't be shy, I shall be disappointed if you leave anything on the tables; what you cannot eat now, put into your pockets and take it back to camp with you. Remember, boys, you are as welcome here today as any guest has ever been. But for you boys we should not have such lovely places as this today.' When he had finished there was hardly a dry eye amongst the ladies.

When we had finished dining we filed out to the lawn in front of the hotel and, while we smoked and munched chocolates, the hotel orchestra entertained us for an hour. Then our titled hosts drove us back again to camp in their luxurious cars, with our pockets full of cigarettes and sweets of all kinds.

For three months I stayed at Summerdown Camp and I do believe I could have been there longer if the desire to go home and see my parents had not taken possession of me. The commandant of the camp was a thorough gentleman and only marked me fit after I had begged him to do so. The three happy months at Eastbourne had made me almost fit again, just a little shortwinded when running and climbing. I left the camp for home on ten days' leave, arriving home just about one year after leaving it at the start of the war. I leave you to imagine the greeting of parents and friends and the joy of that ten days, and then the parting again as my leave expired and I made my way to the reserve unit of my regiment at Hull.[17]

I had not been here long when I was given the post of assistant to the sergeant of military police, being billeted in the police station, the civilian and military police working together for the discipline in the town. My duty was mainly to run errands and carry messages for the sergeant, but I saw and learned a lot during this time. The sergeant would parade the streets at night with a party of twenty or thirty men and often return with drunken soldiers, sometimes with deserters, throwing them into the cells. At weekends I was surprised to see the number of men and women the civilian police would drag to the station and throw into the cells, the cursing and swearing and vulgar language being awful to hear. Then, the following morning, what a sight – the dishevelled and unwashed prisoners, the stinking cell, the gaudy and foul-mouthed prostitutes; and this was just one night's catch.

My job here also was to conduct and safely deliver batches of prisoners at Hessle jail. I had to take them by tramcar to Hessle and see them safely inside. I was generally in charge of about a dozen or twenty of these prisoners, who were going to serve sentences of from fourteen days to six months. I never enjoyed this job and felt sorry for the boys when they got through the great locked doors and came under the strict discipline inside the jail. As we entered the jail grounds and looked up at the prisoners' quarters, hands stuck out through the iron bars and waved to us, those already in recognising some pal just arriving. This was a jail where capital punishment was carried out but I had no wish to explore it and felt much better when the warder on the huge gates clanged them behind me. According to the boys it wasn't a very healthy place to stay in.

Anyhow, this job was too nice and easy for me, or else the authorities decided that, with my knowledge of real warfare, I would be more useful at the front again, and promptly marked me to return to my unit at Sutton Village. Into strict training I was soon put again, and very shortly after my name once more appeared on a draft for France.

4

Gallipoli and Egypt

Dissatisfaction with the progress of the war on the Western Front encouraged Allied leaders to launch an attack on Turkey, with the intention of 'knocking the props' from beneath Germany. Opinion at the time was divided as to the wisdom of the project, and there has been little subsequent agreement amongst historians, some of whom support the 'Westerners', arguing that it was only in France that the war could be won, while others support the 'Easterners' in their desire to find a more profitable theatre of operations.

Whatever the theorectical attractions of a landing on Gallipoli, there is little doubt that the campaign was badly handled. Initial allied landings on 25 April 1915 met with some success, but the pattern of the Western Front soon re-established itself, with the trench warfare of artillery and machine gun bringing movement to a halt. A fresh landing on 6 August made some promising gains, but unenterprising generalship, difficult terrain and resolute Turkish defence brought it too to a halt. The campaign grew increasingly costly, consuming men and munitions originally destined for France.

By this time the Dardanelles campaign had begun and troops were wanted there. Having had one dose in the Flanders trenches, I approached the officer in charge to put me on a draft to Gallipoli. My request was granted. I was given six days' draft leave and made the best of such a short time. Again the heartbreaking goodbyes of relatives and friends, then back at Sutton.

Soon after getting back I had to parade at the medical room and receive two inoculations, which put me off colour for a day or two.

On the night before we were due to leave for Gallipoli the whole draft was put into the village schoolroom, with orders that no man would be allowed out that evening. The boys considered this treatment rotten – quite a few, including myself, having been to France already. So a little conference in a corner of the schoolroom soon decided what action was to be taken. A sudden rush to the door, the military police who guarded the door knocked down, and away to town all who felt inclined, on a last fling.

What about the consequences of such conduct? Well, what did men who had spent winter in the trenches of Flanders care about prison cells? Weren't they awfully good dug-outs? Anyhow, when the roll was called the following morning every man had returned, even if not yet properly sober, and the officer in command, although reluctantly forgiving, knew that sufficient punishment would be coming to these men very soon. So away to the station we marched, shaking hands as we went along and receiving the best wishes of relatives, friends and pals. Settled in the train in the little village station, we leaned out of the carriage windows waiting for the off, singing popular war songs along with the crowd on the platform. Then the train began to move out of the station, someone called for 'three cheers for Captain so-and-so' – a decent fellow. Then someone called for 'three boos for Major so-and-so' – described as a slave-driver, a coward, a pig, and several other names not fit to mention. Amidst a tumult of cheers and jeers the train drew away from Sutton.

Late that afternoon we arrived at Devonport, where we left the train and marched to a temporary embarkation camp, just outside the town. Here we sorted ourselves out into the huts and had tea. While having tea we were told that we would embark in the morning, and also that we would be allowed out into town that evening if we wished to go. Any man failing to put in an appearance at roll call in the morning would be posted as a deserter as if from active service. Some of the men went in for a real last fling, and all through the night they were crawling back to camp.

Next day we marched off to the boat. She was a good-sized two-funneled steamer called the *Northland*.[18] Once aboard we were all told off to our different beds and messes, and given a lifebelt, which we were told must always be with us. In fact it would be a crime to be caught without it during any moment of the journey.

Our quarters were quite comfortable. The beds were wire-netting racks with straw palliasses and pillows, in two rows one above the other below the hatches in the forward part of the ship. The officers and higher NCOs, of course, had the cabins and bunks. We had plenty of blankets, which we would certainly need for a while, it was October and as we had marched to the boat it had snowed hard and a bitter cold wind was blowing up on deck. At dinner time we had our first meal on the boat. The food was good and sufficient. Men were detailed off to assist the ship's cook and do the washing up after meals.

It was on the twenty-sixth day of October that we sailed from Devonport bound for Gallipoli. Two destroyers accompanied us for the first day, and then turned about and left us to look after ourselves. This dampened our spirits a little as we thought they would accompany us all the way. The first night on board I hardly slept. I was feeling a little seasick and I lay on my bed staring at the deck a few inches above my head and listening to the throb of the boat's engines wondering too what fate had in store for me on my second trip to the front. The boys were fairly quiet too. I suppose they were feeling something like I was. I knew what a dangerous journey we were on, and I hoped and prayed that we would steer clear of those death-dealing submarines.

Almost by dawn I was up on deck. It was very cold and the sea was very rough, and quite unconsciously I kept a good look-out for periscopes. That day we were all detailed off either to lifeboats or rafts. Two men were told off as guards to each boat, their duty being to see that in case of fire or being torpedoed the men entered their boats in orderly fashion, the two guards to be the last persons to enter the boat. Machine guns were fixed on the top deck, fore and aft of the ship, the gunners having orders to fire at once on anything resembling a submarine periscope. Almost each day we had a practice alarm, the alarm signal being short, sharp blasts on the ship's siren. On hearing this signal, every man rushed instantly to his boat or raft, and remained there until the all-clear signal went.

But on we sailed without incident on the fringe of the Bay of Biscay, feeling the swell of that famous bay. We were expecting soon to come in sight of Gibraltar, but rumour got about on board that we had been warned to approach Gib by a circular route because of enemy submarines lying on our track. I don't know how true this rumour was, but we eventually sailed into the straits of Gib at night. I could just see the faint outline of the great rock, with its myriad lights gleaming on it. Then the beam of a great searchlight found our ship and more beams were turned on us, the brilliant light almost blinding me.

There was our ship in the straits, reminding one of the artiste on the stage of a darkened theatre with all the spotlights of the wings turned on her. Also I noticed that our ship had considerably slackened her speed and the sailors were quickly running up flag signals, which of course I did not understand. Then I noticed a smart naval launch making for the ship. It came right alongside; a rope ladder was dropped over the side to it, and the next minute a naval officer of some kind climbed on board and went straight to the captain's cabin. What this officer's mission was I don't know, but after a little while he returned to the launch, which put off again to the shore, and our ship went full speed ahead again into the Mediterranean Sea. We were still without escort, but the searchlight of a destroyer would suddenly find us, remain on us for a few moments and then leave us in the darkness again.

When daylight came we found that we were sailing in sight of land. Someone said we had received orders to sail along the North African coast and we could plainly see the hilly country and white buildings of Morocco and Algeria shining in the sunlight.

The weather was quite nice and warm now, in contrast with a few days before when we had embarked at Devonport, shivering in the cold wind and sleet. The boys all lay about the deck in their shirt-sleeves, some writing letters, some reading books and others playing different gambling games. As I leaned over the rail looking down into the truly blue Mediterranean and watching the various marine animals swimming about I could hear the familiar cry of 'Who says a bit more on the dirty old mudhook?' and the old 'clickety-click', 'Kelly's legs', 'Kelly's eye', etc., as the games of Crown and Anchor and Housey-Housey proceeded.

Each morning we paraded on deck in our stockinged feet, with pants braced up, for half an hour's gymnastics, thoroughly enjoying the fun of doing one-legged balancing exercises as the ship rolled to the swell. One night a great hospital ship hove into sight on her way to England with her human cargo of sick and wounded. I thought she looked beautiful with the scores of green lights running along her deck rail right round the ship, and the great illuminated red cross amidships, reaching from the top deck to the dark waves lapping her sides. Surely no submarine commander could mistake the mission of such a ship. The boys came up from below to have a look at her, and as she passed we gave her a cheer, an answering cheer and shouts of 'good luck' coming back from her across the dark water.

Then down again on to our beds, to hear a good solo or a duet, or to join in singing popular songs. Also a few stories – whether clean or dirty didn't matter much – until the gentle swing of the ship sent us into dreamland.

The following morning there was no land to be seen. We had altered our course for the middle of the Mediterranean. Shoals of porpoises came bounding to meet us, then swam along with the ship, their round, plump bodies leaping along as if playing leap-frog with the waves. All at once the voice of the look-out man up in the crow's-nest above us bawled out, 'Land ahead, Sir.' There was a rush for the forecastle rail and soon the faint outline of land could be seen. We were looking at the island of Malta. As we approached Malta a destroyer came out to meet us, and apparently to guide us into the harbour. Everyone was on deck now and our ship filed her way between British and French warships, the crews giving us a cheer, and a naval band on a large French cruiser played 'Tipperary' and the 'Marseillaise'.

As soon as we dropped anchor our ship was beseiged by small boats, loaded with fruit, cigarettes and silks, the Maltese in the boats clamouring for us to buy. They threw up to the deck a rope line, to which was attached a basket, the boys catching the line and doing business by winding the basket up and down.

Standing in a small rowing boat close to our ship was a tall Maltese dressed in a swimming costume. He kept repeating parrotwise, 'See her dive, see her dive, other side, one shilling, one shilling other side.' For one shilling, which was soon thrown down to him, this man dived under our ship, coming up at the other side after what seemed an eternity to me. This was no mean feat, I believe. Also calling out 'See her dive' from a small boat no bigger than a house bath were two small boys, naked, one or the other continually bailing out their old boat with a jam tin. Down into the water we threw coppers, cap badges, buttons, and the two little fellows were diving into the water and swimming like ducks, retrieving these articles before they had sunk very far. Suddenly they would row off as fast as they could, as the harbour police launch came steaming up, to return again with the cry of 'See her dive' as soon as the police got past our ship.

Next day we sailed off again once more without escort. The weather was beautiful and the sea a lovely blue. I leaned over the rail and watched the flying fish skim along over the water, to suddenly disappear again into a wave caused by the wash of the ship. During the night I enjoyed watching the fish swim round about the ship, their phosphorous bodies showing them quite plainly in the dark sea. What a glorious sail it was! One almost forgot the war and the deadly submarine which might have been lurking near to us at that very moment. For now we were in the dangerous Aegean Sea and would soon be sailing amongst the scores of small islands and rocks of the Greek Archipelago where only a fortnight before the troopship *Royal Edward* had been sent to the bottom by a German torpedo, and hundreds of soldiers sailing in her had been drowned.

It was quite plain to all on our ship that this sea was a beautiful haunt for submarines. A sharper look-out was kept now. The alarm was sounded more frequently. Every man was ordered to sleep on deck during the night, using his lifebelt as a pillow. Strict orders were issued that no man must strike a light or smoke on deck. Sentries were posted, with orders to shoot at once any man disobeying these orders. Silence was also essential, and singing or loud talking was also forbidden. Of course, in spite of the obvious danger of striking a match, the boys didn't do without the old fag. Where there's a will, there's a way, and down under a couple of blankets the boys had a few whiffs in their turns.

During the day dead horses or mules often came floating by the ship, having been thrown overboard from some horse transport gone on in front of us. One morning the whole ship had the wind up when what surely appeared to be the glass of a periscope flashed in the sunlight. The alarm sounded, and every man stood by his boat, alert and waiting to see what would happen. The ship altered her course, and the gun, which was aft of the ship, was turned on to this shining object, the gunners ready to blaze away for life, but the excitement was soon cooled down and a feeling of relief went through the ship when the captain had the 'All right' signal given and shouted down to us from the bridge that the object that had caused so much commotion was only a biscuit tin thrown carelessly overboard and floating along. The ship was turned back on to her right course, and coming close up to the biscuit tin the officers amused themselves shooting at it until it sank.

One night as we lay in our blankets on deck, some sleeping and others lying staring up at the stars that shone in the sky line like diamonds, the

1 *George Ashurst (standing, right) on annual training in
1913.*

2 *The village of Le Touquet, winter 1914. This photograph is taken from C Company's forward barricade on the Frelinghien road, looking back towards the British lines.*

3 *Survivors of the 1st Lancashire Fusiliers manning trenches near Mouse Trap Farm after the gas attack of 2 May 1915. Note the improvised respirators.*

4   George Ashurst as a corporal, convalescing in Eastbourne, 1915.

5 *SS* Zeeland (*formerly* Northland).

6 *Lancashire Landing, W Beach at Cape Helles. The 1st Lancashire Fusiliers suffered heavily landing here on 25 April 1915. Ashurst came ashore on the nearby V Beach eight months later.*

7 *Mudros Harbour, 1915.*

8   *This photograph purports to show C Company the 1st Lancashire Fusiliers on the morning of 1 July 1916. Ashurst suggests, however, that it was taken some days previously.*

9 The explosion of the mine beneath the Hawthorn Redoubt, 7.20 a.m., 1 July 1916.

10 This photograph, taken from the forward positions of the 1st Lancashire Fusiliers, shows troops to the Fusiliers' right – either the 2nd Royal Fusiliers or the 16th Middlesex – falling back. It may well be the 'sudden retirement' at 9.45 a.m. to which the Lancashire Fusiliers' War Diary refers, and which so alarmed Ashurst.

11   Colonel Nissen in front of a Nissen Hut, Blagny 1917.

12   The Nieuport sector, July 1917.

voice of the look-out man in the crow's-nest up above us rang out –
'Light ahead, Sir.' Immediately most of the boys sprang up and ran to
the forecastle rail, peering ahead through the darkness. A few moments
later the voice of the officer on duty on the bridge answered 'Aye, aye'.
Then shortly ahead of us appeared a red light, coming nearer and nearer.
This light again caused a great deal of excitement and the general
question amongst the boys was: will it be friend or foe? In a few minutes
we were soon to know.

A brilliant light enveloped our ship, and as our eyes got used to it,
looking across on the starboard side we saw a great grey cruiser. Our ship
had stopped her engines now and we waited for the next thing to happen.
We had not long to wait. Across the water floated a stentorian voice
saying, 'Who are you?' Back from our ship went the answer, 'HMT
Northland, Sir.' Again the voice from the cruiser demanded, 'Where are
you bound for?' and again the answer, 'Mudros, Sir.' 'What have you got
aboard?' came again the deep voice through the megaphone, our answer
being 'Troops, Sir'. Then came the last word and order from the cruiser:
'All right, *Northland*, follow me through the night.' 'Aye, aye, Sir,'
answered our officer on the bridge.

During this midnight conversation between the two ships the boys
stood silently staring across the water at the great grey broadside of the
cruiser, her great guns looking as if they were eagerly waiting for the
order to blow us off the face of the sea. But on hearing the last order from
the cruiser we knew she was a good old British boat, and as she turned
about and took up a position about half a mile in front of us we settled
down on deck under our blankets to sleep, feeling quite safe now with
the good old navy lads close at hand.

Morning dawned again and with it the voice of the look-out man rang
out again – 'Land ahead, Sir.' The usual rush to the forecastle rail
followed and soon we could see the faint outline of land. Our escort of
the night was there, sailing steadily on in front of us, then as our ship
appeared to be only a few miles from the land the cruiser turned about,
and as she slowly steamed past us we heard the familiar megaphoned
voice of the night call out, 'Goodbye *Northland*, and good luck', and the
lads in blue gave us three hearty British cheers. Then as three great
answering cheers rang out from our ship and died away in the breeze the
cruiser sailed away to bring some other ship safely through that
dangerous sea.

In front of us now lay the island of Lemnos. From the sea it did not
appear a very beautiful isle; it looked barren and hilly, with great canvas
camps dotted here and there on its slopes. It had a large harbour, across
which at even distances were large floats. These floats, I was told,
supported sunken submarine nets, and the one and only opening
through these nets and floats was the secret entrance to the harbour,

known only to a very few naval officers. As we slowly approached the harbour a small, well polished steam launch came out to meet us. Out of its very cosy little cabin stepped a naval officer with quite a lot of gold braid about his uniform. He asked who we were and what we were, and was answered very politely from the bridge by the captain. 'Come along,' said the gold braid 'and I will show you your berth.' Chugging away, the trim little launch led the way into the harbour, and slowly we followed on. We sailed by dozens of ships of almost every kind anchored in the harbour – great battleships, great liners, hospital ships, tramp steamers, submarines, and all sorts of river and canal boats – eventually dropping anchor near a large steamship which was painted all white. This ship, I understand, was the army headquarters for the Dardanelles operations.[19] Further across the harbour was berthed a cruiser with extra tall wireless masts, which was the naval headquarters.

We were all anxious to be getting ashore now, after eleven days on board, but for some reason we did not land for another two days. We did not mind this a great deal, seeing that we were quite comfortable and quite safe now from the dreaded torpedos, and to improve matters we were paid out, and lots of provisions were brought aboard for us to buy. We had quite a jolly time, lounging about the deck, having a hand at cards, eating tinned fruits and biscuits, and enjoying the evening concerts, our own artistes supplemented by other artistes from the shore and other ships.

Eventually orders came round to prepare to disembark, and all sorts of small craft came alongside our ship to transport us to the shore. I just managed to get a footing on a small paddle boat that had sailed for years on the River Nile in Egypt. We were so crowded on these little boats that if one man had sneezed a dozen men would have been cannoned into the water. Slowly we were carried to a half-constructed stone pier, which, from the jokes of the men around me, reminded me of my home town, Wigan. Carefully we climbed ashore and formed up into marching order. Then we moved off to the camp that was to be our home until we were required in the trenches on Gallipoli.

As we marched along we passed huge ammunition and ration dumps, also large canvas hospitals in which scores of men lay with that horrid disease, dysentery. Working on the roads over which we marched were hundreds of men and boys of what nationality I did not know. I had never seen such specimens of humanity in my life before. They sat on their haunches grinning at us as we marched by, dirty, lousy, unshaven, scratching themselves for all they were worth, dressed in the most comical fashion, some of them wearing the dirty, holey underpants thrown off by some soldier who could not bear the bite of the lice in them. Others were wearing old worn-out tunics on top of their long Greek robes, with a badly battered hat to set them off. I was told that lots of these creatures died in their sleep at night and I could quite believe it. I am sure their bodies were just incubators for disease. I was glad when we passed the last of them; the sight almost made me sick.

After marching about four miles we arrived at our divisional base camp. We were detailed off to tents and told to parade again next morning at 8 for a lecture. Our camp was pitched on the side of a hill, the ground being very sandy and dry. Below us in the distance we could see Mudros Bay, where we had disembarked. All round about us were great camps filled with reinforcements for Gallipoli.

There were a great number of Australians and New Zealanders on the island. It was the first time I had come into contact with these colonials and I was surprised at their free and easy discipline, only being used to the rigid discipline of the British Army. Perhaps they had a little swagger with them but then I think they were entitled to that because they had six times as much money per day as we had, and they used to say, 'Only a bob a day Tommy – why don't you go on strike for more money?' Anyhow, a lot of them were very free with their money, as the following incident will show.

I and three of my pals were sitting outside our tent one afternoon, just going to have tea of bread and jam. Along came two Aussies making their way to their own camp, one of them carrying over his shoulder a blanket which was fairly heavily loaded from a visit to the canteen. Looking down at us as he was passing, he said, 'Hello Lancs, going to have tea? What are you having?' Seeing the jam tin he said, 'Bread and sandy possey? That only means darned dysentery. Have a good tuck in at my expense' – and so saying he tipped the blanket from his back, emptying the whole contents on to the sand at our feet. Then, carelessly wrapping up the blanket again, he turned to his pal and said, 'Well, Pard, we've got to go and fill this again now.' At our feet lay tins of sardines and fruit, packets of biscuits and cigarettes, and that afternoon we had the best tea we had had for some time and were likely to have for some time to come.

The island was inhabited by Greeks. Their houses were poor buildings made of stone and the villages very insanitary and ancient. Fruit and nuts and oranges grew on the island and were fairly cheap to buy, or would have been cheap if the wily villagers had not learned the art of profiteering. Their drinking water they got from wells, carrying it in big earthenware jugs on their shoulders. The ladies wore long dresses down to their ankles and were without shoes and stockings. One young lady in particular that came to the well daily was a real Grecian beauty. She wore a long crimson dress and her jet-black hair reached down to her calves. The boys called her 'the lady of the well' and often gangs of the boys would have a walk to the well just to gaze on her. Perhaps one would volunteer to carry the water for her, but one fiery look from those serpent-like eyes was enough to discourage even a Tommy on active service.

Our work on the island consisted of route marches, sham fighting, and fatigues, but I am sure the training was not as severe as it was at the bases in Flanders.

Dysentery was the curse of the island, the hospitals overflowing with these cases. Dozens died daily, the sound of the Last Post seemed to echo the whole day through from the huge cemetery on the hill above the camp. No matter what precautions we took with our food, every time I had anything to eat I had the horrible sensation of chewing sand. If the wind blew at all the sand blew about in clouds, filling our eyes, nose and mouth. One could see only a few feet ahead during these sand storms, the flying sand cutting and stinging the face painfully. When it rained it came down in torrents, stopping again as suddenly as it started, and leaving only the rivulets in the sand to show it had rained at all.

Our latrines were just long trenches dug in the ground, with a wall of canvas around them. It was quite common for some poor fellow to sit at these places for hours at a time, and sometimes die there, another victim of dysentery.

Looking down from our tent during the evening into the valley below one could see hundreds of twinkling lights, with dark shadows moving about them. These lights were from hundreds of candles stuck into the sand around scores of gambling boards of every description. This spot was known to the boys as Monte Carlo. Hundreds of pounds changed hands here nightly, at every kind of game of chance. To visit this Monte Carlo on pay night was a sight and experience not to be forgotten.

A beautiful evening, the stars shining brilliantly overhead, not a breath of wind to cause a flicker even of a flame of one of the hundreds of candles. Warm enough to sit on the sand around the gambling boards. The Crown and Anchor man sat in his shirt-sleeves, his hat beside him full of notes and silver, throwing the dice, paying out and collecting in as he shouted the familiar 'Who says a bit more on the dirty old mudhook?', his forehead wet with perspiration from the excitement of the game, the men sitting and lying round about the board, silently placing their money on their fancy. Now and then one of these men would rise and walk back to camp, flushed with luck and winnings, only to return again the next evening to learn how fickle is the goddess of chance.

In the regimental canteens beer was sold to the troops, but each man was only allowed two pints daily, one at dinner time and one in the evening. During this beer issue it was quite common to see a queue a quarter of a mile long, stretching from the canteen, the military police keeping the men in order and doing their best to stop men from coming the 'double'. The beer was not of a very good quality, but the boys said there could be no bad beer in a place like Mudros.

In a couple of weeks' time we had regained our land legs and were somewhat acclimatised, and the order came around to pack up for service on Gallipoli, which was about six hours' sail away. Down to the bay we marched, climbing on to small barges at the pierhead which took us out to the steamers which were to take us up the line.

The ship I sailed on was called the *Robin Redbreast*. We sailed out of the harbour during the evening so as to arrive at Gallipoli in the darkness of the night. While on our way we passed huge battleships that were shelling the Turkish lines at long range, sometimes passing what appeared to be battleships without the usual complement of cheering sailors. These ships were old liners painted the dull grey of a warship and camouflaged to look like warships, with huge tree trunks arranged on her decks like big guns ready for action. These were decoy ships used to draw the enemy's fire and submarine attacks on to a false target.[20]

We learned on board that our destination was to be Suvla Bay, the place of a second landing, on the west coast of the peninsula. During the night our ship dropped anchor about a mile from the coast. Small oil-driven barges came like shadows alongside the ship. We were ordered to get into these quietly, and without lights of any description. We got right down into the holds of these little iron boats, packed as usual like sardines, and away chugged the barges to the beach.

Silently climbing ashore, we formed up into something like single file and moved off in the darkness. We passed huge dumps of what looked like ammunition and ration boxes. Soon we were in the open country and odd shells from Johnny Turk came over, luckily hurting no one. We walked on silently behind one another, not having the least idea how far we had to go, or what was round about us, simply following the guide who had come down from the regiment to the beach to meet us. Eventually we turned into a gully and in front of us, a little distance ahead, we noticed a lot of small, twinkling lights. As we got nearer to the lights, dark figures came to meet us, and from the enquiries from pals and other greetings we knew we had reached the battalion which had just come out of the front line for a couple of days in the reserves. The men had made the sides of the gully into great steps on which they had built small dug-outs, the whole affair in the daytime looking like a lot of flats in a cave-man's dwelling-place.

Having served in France with the 2nd Battalion, Ashurst now found himself joining his regiment's other regular battalion, the 1st. This had been at Karachi on the outbreak of war and, spent the early part of 1915 in England, leaving for Egypt on 15 March as part of the 29th Division's 86th Infantry Brigade. On 25 April the battalion earned undying glory when it went ashore on W beach – 'Lancashire Landing' – at Gallipoli. Eleven officers and 350 men were killed or wounded during the landing itself, and by the end of the day only 11 officers and 399 men were still fit for duty. Six Victoria Crosses were awarded to Lancashire Fusiliers for gallantry that day.

The battalion suffered severely in the trench warfare that followed, and on the night of

26 – 7 November a savage storm resulted in 20 men being drowned, at least 19 frozen to death, and 11 officers and 525 men evacuated sick. It was under these inauspicious circumstances that Ashurst reached the battalion near Suvla Bay.

We found the battalion very weak in numbers, a monsoon a few days before we arrived having wiped out half the battalion, men being actually drowned in the trenches and others having gone into hospital with frostbite. Having been detailed off to different companies, we fixed up as best we could for the remainder of the night in the dug-outs available. Then, when daylight came, we set about making homes for ourselves.

During the morning I had a good look round and noticed other gullies with different regiments billeted in them, looking right down the gully. I could see the beach and bay where we had landed the previous night. Down on the beach was a big canvas hospital, the great red cross showing plainly on the while marquees, and anchored in the bay was a hospital ship. A couple of monitors lay a little further out to sea, backed up by two cruisers.

I could sit by my dug-out in the daytime and watch the monitors, which were little boats with a big gun, fire at the Turkish positions and them quickly move their own position, causing the Turkish gunners great difficulty in sighting their guns, thereby dropping their shells harmlessly into the water, sending up great fountains of water. These monitors and cruisers were, of course, our big artillery, and when the cruisers let Johnny Turk have a broadside the deafening noise reverberated up the gully in which we lived and a great cloud of black smoke enveloped the ship.

Very soon it came time to go into the trenches. We found the front very quiet and we spent the time in between sentry duty building up the trench and improving our dug-outs. We had not done much trench duty on Suvla Bay when the rumour got around that we were going to evacuate the place. This rumour didn't seem at all probable: everywhere we were strengthening our defences and using quite a large number of new sandbags. We could see away behind the front line the Royal Signalling Corps putting up brand-new telephone wires, and field guns were moving up from the beach into new positions.[21] In fact, I thought myself that a new offensive was about to be launched at the Turks.

However, one afternoon we were told to pack all our kit ready to move. That night we stood in the gully in the darkness; only whispered conversations were going on, and an officer's torchlight flashed now and again just for a moment. The order for complete silence and no lights whatever was whispered along the lines.

Looking down towards the beach we could see the great hospital, lit up more brilliantly than ever, and in the bay rested two hospital ships, all brilliantly lit up in their colours of green and red. Now and again a field gun would bark out, sending over to Johnny Turk an 18 pound souvenir, and a machine gun would pitter-patter for a few moments, to be followed by the sharp crack of a sniper's rifle. Surely we could not be leaving this place and sneaking away like a thief in the night. But the order came quietly down the line to move on, and silently, like shadows, we moved down the gully and onto the beach. It didn't seem real that those great piles of boxes were only empty, and that not a sick or wounded man lay in the great hospital, or that dawn would tell Johnny Turk that he was alone on Suvla.

Once again we packed ourselves into the little iron barges, and heaved a sigh of relief as we felt the little oil engine vibrate through the boat and draw us away from the beach. In a few minutes we were alongside the ship again that was to take us from Suvla Bay for ever.

As soon as we were safely on board we enquired where our next destination was, as is always usual for Tommy. No one knew, and we had to be satisfied with guesses. I noticed that our ship was only small and that decided me that our journey would not be far. When all was ready we moved off in the night. We settled down as comfortably as possible, soon procured boiling water to make tea, and enjoyed a meal of tea and bully beef and biscuits, then had a smoke which we had been denied since we left the gully. As we sailed on through the night we discovered that only our company was on the ship, the other three companies of the battalion having embarked on other ships.

As daylight broke we looked around and to our surprise we found ourselves once again entering Mudros Bay. This time our little steamer sailed alongside a big liner which had a terrible list to one side. We climbed aboard her when ordered and could walk on her deck only with difficulty, the slope being such an acute angle. We were told to make ourselves comfortable on her and await further orders. Very soon we discovered the ship's name was *Southland*, a sister ship to *Northland*, in which I had sailed from England. It appeared that she had been torpedoed but had managed to reach harbour. There was a nasty hole in her starboard side and she still held a lot of water. A few naval divers and repairers were aboard her, patching her up temporarily, until she could get into dry dock back in England.[22]

During the daytime we were quite interested watching these naval divers at work, and often assisted in working the air and water pumps. We thought it very strange to be dumped on a crippled liner but we found out that it was all through some mistake. The other three companies of our battalion had left Suvla Bay and gone right on to Cape Helles, the main landing on Gallipoli, while our company, through a misunderstanding, had sailed back to Mudros. This state of affairs made it very awkward for us. Our rations were, of course, with the battalion and we were stranded six hours' sail away from them. Anyhow, we made the best of our time on the wounded liner, playing cards and arranging little concerts in the evening to while away the time as pleasantly as possible, living on our iron rations, bully beef and biscuits, and what other food our officers could beg for us from other units on shore.

After a week on the *Southland* they found a little ship to take us to Gallipoli. In the darkness of night we landed on that famous beach where my battalion had made that glorious landing on the morning of 25 April, about eight months before. As we walked to the communications trenches a shell from Johnny Turk exploded on the beach, giving us a momentary glimpse of our surroundings and also reminding us that once again we were in the danger zone.

After winding along what seemed a never-ending trench, and without any untoward incident, we reached the reserve trenches, and here found the remainder of our battalion, acting as reserves and mostly supplying working parties to carry ammunition to the front line and build up defences, the battalion being too weak in numbers to be a fighting unit. Anyhow, we soon settled down in the little corrugated iron-roofed dug-outs allotted to us for the night, and when daylight came we took stock of our surroundings and had a good look round.

Right in front of us was that battered and famous ridge, Achi-Baba, and on both sides and behind us was the sea – at least, on our right were the Dardenelles straits. Swift torpedo boats and destroyers ceaselessly patrolled the coast, ready instantly to tackle the wily submarine should one attempt to attack the larger battleships that lay out to sea, shelling the Turkish positions. Immediately behind us lay the steamship *River Clyde*, with her nose resting on the beach, without funnels or masts, just her bare bulk lying there, battered and beaten, like a fallen soldier, but through her 'dead body' still doing wonderful service in giving thousands of British soldiers a safe landing on Gallipoli.[23] Looking down on her were the General Headquarters, built into the face of the cliff up above and facing the sea, absolutely safe from the shells of Johnny Turk. By the beach and just to our right was what remained of the fort of Sedd El Bahr. Her great stone walls had been knocked to pieces, and her guns twisted into scrap iron by the great fifteen-inch guns of *Queen Elizabeth*. There was a huge canvas hospital on the beach, and also canteens where one could buy cups of tea, biscuits, chocolates, cigarettes etc.

When down on the beach for some reason or other, one had to be continually on the alert. From over on the Asian side of the narrows a great gun of the Turks used to shell the beach from about twelve miles' distance. This gun, which did a great deal of damage, killing lots of horses and mules, was known by the boys on Gallipoli as 'Asiatic Annie'. As a special precaution of safety the French, who were on our right, fixed up a look-out man on the highest wall of the fort left standing. Through his powerful glasses he kept a sharp look-out across the narrows and into the desert beyond. On seeing the smoke rise as Asiatic Annie fired and sent her half-ton shell hurtling towards the beach, he gave a long blast on a horn that could be heard all over the beach. Instantly on hearing the horn, everyone dashed for cover, jumping into the trenches specially dug for this purpose. From the sound of the look-out man's horn, twenty seconds elapsed before the great shell came screaming down on the beach. Our monitors and cruisers did their best to silence Asiatic Annie and we often thought they had succeeded when she was quiet for a day or two, but just like the proverbial bad penny she would turn up again when least expected.

Running up from the beach right to the front line was a fine communication trench called 'The Great North Road', along which even donkeys could walk and carry ammunition and rations. Enemy aeroplanes came flying over pretty frequently, dropping bombs and showers of small aerial darts. These small steel darts scattered from an aeroplane at a great height were a nasty little weapon, and trenches were not cover from them so we packed the roof of our shelters about a yard thick with clay and soil for protection, and when an air raid was on we peeped out of our dug-outs and took pot-shots at the enemy aircraft. Surely if ever there was a spot between the devil and the deep sea, our position on Gallipoli was that spot.

Early one evening as we sat in our trench looking out to sea a destroyer which was quite close in to shore suddenly fired three or four quick shots. As we scanned the sea to see what was the cause of this sudden commotion we saw a short distance from the destroyer a great cloud of black smoke rise slowly out of the water. The alert naval gunners had sent one more German U boat to the bottom of the sea.

As the great shells from our battleships moaned overhead to drop on Achi Baba and make one more dent in the already badly dented ridge, rumours began to be whispered around amongst the boys, rumours that I had heard once before on Suvla – rumours of evacuation. Anyhow, we began to dig more trenches down to the beach. Our artillery became more active and the usual strengthening of front-line trenches took place.

Caterpillar tractors could be seen right down on the beach drawing what appeared to be huge guns into position, but which were really nothing more than great tree trunks and barrels well camouflaged. Bombing raids into Johnny Turk's lines at night by the infantry helped to make the enemy believe that an advance was about to be launched, but in the darkness of night loads of all kinds of material and scores of sick and wounded were being taken on to the ships. On the beach, under cover of the cliffs, huge dumps were made of stuff that could not be got away and would be useful to the enemy, the dumps being wired and arranged so that they could be sent sky high at any moment.

During these operations Christmas Day of 1915 came and passed almost unnoticed. Our parcels from home with greetings and dainties did not get to us, and the sacred day passed much like other days.

A few days later the order came round to pack up, and when darkness came we moved down to the beach. By platoons and in single file we walked quietly down the long communication trench. Down on the beach we could feel the suppressed excitement and unconsciously spoke in whispers, also moving quickly to any order given. It seemed incredible that Johnny Turk could remain in his trenches and not be aware that the whole army in front of him was leaving the peninsula, and as we walked across the beach I felt just like a man who is walking across a field in which stands, glaring at him, a fierce bull.

Anyhow, most men, I am sure, heaved a sigh of relief and breathed more freely as we entered the battered hull of the old *River Clyde*. Quickly we walked through this sheltered and ready-made pier to the sea end, where we just as quickly climbed aboard the little boats which took us out to the waiting steamers which had moved fairly close in under cover of darkness to take us away from Gallipoli for ever.[24]

Once on board the strain of the evacuation died down and the boys let themselves go a little and began to sing and joke again. As the ship moved away from that tragic peninsula, leaving behind only the gallant comrades whom Johnny Turk could hurt no more, we saw the great dumps on the beach burst into flame, signalling the end of a battle front that was nothing more than a death trap.

Once again we were on the move and the boys were ignorant of their destination. The powers in charge seemed to take a delight in leaving Tommy guessing, and guess Tommy did! At first it was England we were going to, and then Salonika for more fighting; then it boiled down to Egypt for a rest. However, a few hours' sailing settled the question: for the third time we sailed into Mudros Bay.

The next morning we disembarked and marched about three miles inland, to settle down again under canvas. We had a fine time here; there were no parades worth talking about, and life was just easy going. While here New Year's Day of 1916 dawned. Our Christmas mail, which had been held back because of the evacuation was delivered to us, and what a mail! There were eighty bags of parcels for less than two hundred men.

Our commanding officer gave orders that every parcel belonging to a dead or wounded comrade must be shared out to us. After personal letters had been extracted and taken charge of by an officer, the contents of the parcels were spread out and sorted. What an assortment of things to eat and use there was! The inside of the marquee looked exactly like a miniature Woolworth's store. There was everything for a soldier's taste and comfort that a mother or wife or a sweetheart could think of. Some of the parcels had been badly knocked about and the contents were broken and spoiled, but each man had enough fancy cake and chocolate to last him for weeks. In fact lots of the boys were like 'little Tommy' after the Christmas party, and had to receive the usual dose of castor oil. Our commanding officer also managed to get us a good allowance of beer and himself bought us lots of vegetables and puddings, which made our old army stew into a real good New Year's dinner.

When the time did come to move, after a couple of weeks of this well fed and easy life, we felt much fitter and happier. Then once again we struck camp and marched off down to the bay. Strangely enough, this time we knew that our destination was Egypt, and gladly we embarked for the land of the sphinxes and pyramids.

Soon we were settled down on a decent-sized but rather old-fashioned steamer called the *Seeang Bee*, which was manned mostly with Hindu sailors and had done years of trading in the Indian Ocean. Our quarters on the boat were fairly comfortable for the three days' sail in front of us. Down on the lower deck forward of the ship were quartered 72 Turkish prisoners we were taking with us to Egypt. I, along with twelve men of a guard, were detailed off to take charge of these prisoners during the voyage. A Turkish officer who had also been taken prisoner, but on his honour was given the freedom of the ship, was also made responsible for the conduct of the prisoners, and of course interpreted all orders to them.

They were rather a sulky lot of fellows, but quickly did everything they were told, scrubbing their deck and tables and forms to a snowy white, the Turkish officer walking amongst them while they worked, with a very nasty-looking whip curled on his arm. During the daytime it was my duty to allow a few of these prisoners at a time up on to the deck for a spell to get a breather of fresh air. They gave us no trouble at all during the journey, and very often we slipped them cigarettes to have a smoke. If we could not understand their thanks, we saw the gratitude in their faces. Before taking charge of these prisoners I was given special written instructions by the commanding officer on board. These instructions stated definitely that should the boat catch fire or be torpedoed, these prisoners were to be locked down below and not given the chance even to save themselves. Of course this looked very cruel on the face of it, but the lifeboats on the ship were limited and, after all, war was on and prisoners must inevitably take what was left. However, luckily for these poor fellows we had a pleasant sail to Alexandria, where they were handed over to the military police and my job of guarding them was finished.

We were only a few hours in Alexandria, and I was very disappointed because in one of the hospitals there a pre-war pal of mine was working as orderly. I had not seen him since the start of the war and I knew he would be so delighted if he only knew that I was so near to him. Standing on the quayside near our ship was an RAMC orderly. Quickly getting to him, I asked him if he knew so-and-so, my pal. Yes, he knew him quite well as they worked in the same hospital together. A few hurried words and the fellow was off to bring my pal down to the ship, but, alas, it was not to be; we marched off the *Seeang Bee* and straight on to the train. No sooner were we sat down on the wooden seats than the train moved off into the desert, leaving my pal and his orderly chum racing down to the boat to find me gone, after being so near.

Anyhow, it was a decent ride in the train, and for once we were not too packed. For ten hours we were on the train, passing through cultivated lands and desert, towns and villages. We passed through Tel-el-Kebir and a place with the peculiar name of Zag-Zig. I noticed that the women and oxen seemed to be doing the work in the fields. The villages were very ancient and poor, the houses being nothing more than mud shelters, built haphazard without streets, or lanes, or order of any kind, just the jagged channels between the houses where the water rushed away during the rains.

Here and there we passed a well which was used for irrigation purposes and I felt sorry for the ox which with a sack over its eyes and fastened to a long, horizontal pole, walked round and round turning the wheel carrying the wooden buckets which raised the water. Next came long stretches of sandy desert – nothing to see on either side of the spiked railway track but miles of sand, no railway fencing, just a single track laid on the sandy wastes.

I was thoroughly enjoying the ride, it being my first glimpse of Egypt, and peace and quiet reigned here. Then the train slowed down and, passing between tents and marquees, came to a stop at New Camp, built about a mile outside the town of Suez. This camp was mostly filled with Australians and Indian troops of Gurkha and Sikh regiments. Very soon we were settled in our tents and having a cooler, the weather being pretty hot just now, and watching the native traders quickly putting up their bamboo and wicket stalls within a few yards of our camp. In a very short time we were able to buy eggs, oranges, nuts, tomatoes, Turkish delight, ice cream and lemonade of a good quality and quite cheap.

Still, the boys were all anxious to be off and have a look at Suez, and during the afternoon the commanding officer gave permission for the boys to leave camp until nine o'clock at night. After tea I and a few more of the boys set off for Suez. As we walked along the desert by the Indian soldiers' camp we noticed neat little pieces of carpet laid here and there on the sand. To walk on these little carpets with your boots on was asking for a knife in your back. They were the little holy carpets used by these Mohammedan worshippers during their prayers in the evening, as they knelt down and bowed to the setting sun.

We met dozens of these native soldiers returning from the town, some with live fowls under their arms, and others sucking long pieces of sugar

76

cane, grinning and showing their white teeth. These smart, dusky soldiers greeted us with 'How-di Tommy.'

The town itself was full of Tommies. I think the whole of my battalion was in Suez that night, and of course the Aussies were splashing their money about. The hotels and the gardens in front, and the restaurants, were chock-full of dining and wining Tommies. Others were staggering about the streets, shouting and singing. The boys were certainly relaxing! Every kind of wine and liquor could be bought by the bottle, and the native shops did a roaring trade in silks and brooches, which the boys bought to send home as souvenirs to mothers, wives and sweethearts. There was a picture palace there too, owned by a Frenchman who, during our stay in Suez, arranged concerts and boxing and wrestling matches in his hall for the pleasure of the troops.

The natives did not seem to like the instrusion into their town and sat smoking their hookahs and scowling at us as we passed by. They certainly had no love for us and were not to be trusted. One or two of our boys who visited the town never returned to camp and were never seen again. These dirty, scowling fellows were certainly responsible for their disappearance. Our command must have thought so too, for they issued the order that every man going to town must wear belt and bayonet. During the boys' drinking orgies many of these natives were left bleeding and unconscious for their unfriendly attitude. Often drinking houses were turned into a shambles, arguments arose, tempers flared up, tables were overturned and bottles began to fly through the air alongside whirling belts, while drunken men lurched into the street, cursing and bleeding.

One evening as I sat with a chum having a drink in one of these 'pubs' and listening to a native who, standing on an empty cask, was doing his best to entertain us with a song, half a dozen drink-sodden Aussies lurched into the place. One of them, glaring at the native, bawled out, 'Shut that hole, you dirty nigger', and, drawing a revolver from his belt, shot at the unfortunate black. The poor fellow dropped from the cask bleeding at the shoulder. The proprietor ran to him to help, uttering curses in his native tongue; immediately an English Tommy remonstrated with the Aussie. Then the fun started. The place was very soon in darkness and I and my chum made a mad drive for the door. As we reached the safety of the street we could hear the crash of chairs and tables and the smashing of glasses and bottles mingled with the curses and oaths of drunken, fighting men.

Down the street dashed an officer and his patrol of thirty men, who paraded the streets of the town to keep order and quiet, and very soon a score or so of drunken soldiers were under arrest and being marched back to camp to answer for their conduct when they were sober the following morning.

After getting a skinful of drink the boys usually made their way back to camp via the railway sidings on one side of the town. Here by these railway sidings was the black spot of Suez, a bunch of houses the boys called the 'Rag'. Here lived the 'Bohemian ladies' of Suez. Girls of all nationalities lived here, their names and country printed on boards above the door. Dressed in their prettiest and flimsiest dresses they waited for Tommy. Black girls were there also, smiling and showing their pearly white teeth: these girls, of course, were the favourites of the Indian troops. Brown-skinned Arab girls, smothered in cheap rings, bracelets and beads, were also there, sitting sipping coffee and smoking cigarettes. The houses were furnished only with a chair or two, a table, and a bed, the walls being adorned with an indecent picture or two.

The scenes at the 'Rag' in the evenings were almost unbelievable. Drunken Tommies danced with almost naked girls, no curtains or blinds were drawn to the windows, and every action of these soulless women and their drunken companions could be plainly seen. And so the immoral life went on and the half-crowns of Tommy kept accumulating in the locked iron box beside the bed, until the military police, promptly on the stroke of nine, cleared the whole place, Tommy returning to camp and the female vultures to count their ill-gotten money.

Returning to camp by the legitimate route was always very amusing. One could ride back to camp on a donkey's back for sixpence, and it was great fun to see the boys, absolutely too drunk to walk back to camp, being carried on the old donkey's back, first sliding off one side, and then the other, the old native who owned the donkey doing his best to keep Tommy mounted, and very often getting cursed for his trouble. Then on arrival at the camp no fare would be forthcoming until he had dug up some officer to help him get his sixpence.

One night I and a corporal chum of mine decided to have a ramble round the native quarter of the town and the back streets. Knowing very well that we would not be safe round there, we buckled on our bayonets and took with us a revolver. Off we went, turning into the slums of Suez. The native men glanced at us out of the corners of their eyes and the women walked across to the opposite side of the street to pass us, pulling their black hoods closer over their faces at the same time, their long, black robes reaching down to their bare feet. Glancing through the holes that served as the doors of their mud houses, we saw these women sitting on the straw that covered the floor, only their long, dark fingers with pink fingernails and their black eyes being visible. We just glanced again into the public house, not taking the risk of having a drink, for even if we had been thirsty we didn't want any oriental 'dope', and we both wanted to see who won the war.

Then suddenly we stopped, for a terrifying screaming and wailing

78

began quite close to us. We looked about but could see nothing, only the open door of a place of worship. Looking into this place we saw a few natives on their knees, bowing and praying. Their footwear was placed neatly outside at the door. Quite suddenly one of these natives would jump up off his knees, run to the door and spit outside, then dash quickly back to his prayers. Still the screaming and wailing continued, and we had not found out where it came from.

As we stood there listening to the bloodcurdling sound two Sikh soldiers came up mounted on camels. Noticing how puzzled we were, they stopped and pointed up to the roof of the building, and there silhouetted against the sky and standing in a kind of railed pulpit was a figure in a long white robe. The figure was waving its arms wildly and uttering the terrifying screams, ending up with a long, dismal wail. As we stood there watching this ghostly figure and listening to its awful scream to Allah, one of the worshipping natives came out of the Mosque and, passing by one of the Sikh soldier's camels, spat on it and then ran away. The Sikh uttered a curse, slithered quickly from the camel's back, whipped a gleaming dagger from his belt and quickly vanished into the darkness to avenge the insult. I and my chum then decided to move on, not wanting to be a witness to murder, or to be mixed up in a mêlée with the natives.

As we walked back to camp under the brilliant stars we heard the bullfrogs barking like great dogs as they sat on the huge leaves of the water lily plant, jumping into the water with a big splash as we approached. Back again in camp we picked our way through the lines of sleeping soldiers to our own blankets and equipment. But one did not want to sleep under blankets or in tents on these lovely evenings, and the boys just undressed and lay down on top of their blankets, leaving the tent flaps and curtains laced up.

But if one could be on sentry at dawn looking down these long lines of sleeping men a miraculous change would be seen to take place. At that time in the early morning an icy cold mist descended onto the almost naked sleeping figures and, wakening up at its chilly touch, the shivering figures suddenly jumped up, dashed into the tent, and curled up in blankets and overcoats, the lines being cleared in a few minutes as if by magic.

Our work at New Camp consisted of physical training, drill, lectures and route marches, these latter being of about six miles' distance, the heat of the day and the loose sand making such a march very hard work. Huge baths were made for us in which we could dive and have a lovely cooler after undertaking one of these marches. The baths were simply great holes dug in the sand and lined with tarpaulin sheets, then filled with water. During the evening while it was cool we played football, matches being arranged with other regiments in the vicinity, and also with teams from naval boats that were in port. We had a real happy time at Suez, the food also being good and plentiful. Of course in such a hot country our meat ration was mutton, and we got a good deal of vegetables.

But the war was still going on and we were required for further active service. Orders came round to strike camp and pack up, ready to move across the Suez Canal and into the desert beyond. Johnny Turk was again contemplating an attack on the canal and Egypt, and we were to stop him.

We marched off to the canal and crossed it by means of a long boat that stretched from one bank to the other and was swung round just like a swing-bridge. Trenches were dug on the banks of the canal and barbed wire entanglements fixed in front of them. We settled down on the Sinai Desert in front of these defences. Here we had the usual drill and parades, sometimes going down to the canal to bathe and sometimes, during our leisure hours, paying a visit to the camel lines which were close by. We used to chat to the huge Australian who was in charge of the camels and were quite interested in the way he managed the sick and unruly ones, and also the wild African natives who fed and cleaned the animals. These natives were very lazy, but the big Aussie kept them going all right with a very nasty-looking whip. We kept well away from the sick camels. These creatures, although seemingly docile enough when well, are apt to be very vicious when ill and a bite with those big yellow teeth almost surely meant serious consequences.

During the mornings when the Sinai Desert mirage quivered on the sand it was very funny looking into the distance. Troops appeared to be wading about up to their waists in water, and only the top halves of tents could be seen, looking like big white cones floating on a placid lake. The thing looked so real that one almost expected to see the splash as someone dived into the smooth surface. No wonder that thirsty desert travellers, and even camels, had been deceived and tormented by this natural phenomenon.

As a little pastime when not on duty we strolled along the desert, turning over stones and seaching for scorpions, being careful not to get stung by this very dangerous insect, knowing full well the pain and the danger of its poison. We also kept a look-out for centipedes, and then we placed these two terrible enemies inside a glass bottle and watched the deadly combat.

When night fell and we curled up in our blankets and lay down on our groundsheets on the sandy desert staring up at the cloudless sky and the brilliant stars, and waiting for sleep to come to us, two glaring searchlights would suddenly sweep their bright beams across our prone forms. These were the headlights of some ship sailing slowly along the canal, and as she negotiated the bends the searchlights shining far ahead of her swept the desert with a dazzling light. Looking towards the canal as this went on one perceived what looked like a great illuminated dragon crawling slowly across the desert; or the ship with her portholes ablaze with light, reminded me of one of my native Lancashire cotton mills being moved slowly and bodily across the desert in the night.

After a week stationed by the canal we gathered up our belongings once again and rode out on the trucks of a narrow gauge railway into the desert about four miles to the railhead, then by platoons and in fours we marched on another three miles. A string of camels followed on behind us, carrying blankets, tents, cooking utensils and rations. Here on the sandy waste the four companies of the battalion settled down as outposts about a mile apart. My company's outpost was right on the very track which was used by the Mohammedans on their pilgrimage to Mecca. Of course there was no beaten track on this shifting sand, but to mark the way great cairns of stones were spread across the desert.

Soon we were digging circular holes in the sand about a yard deep and large enough to hold a tent when pitched. By pitching our camp in this fashion our tents were mostly hidden from the enemy's view and when the sandstorms came we retired into the tents, lacing them up and shutting out the blinding, flying sand. Round the outpost we dug a trench, using wire netting and sacking to build up the walls of loose sand. We also put out a ring of barbed wire entanglements a few yards from the trench. One sandstorm would amost bury our tents, and after shovelling our way out we would find our trench full up to the top. We were just like sailors in a leaky boat; the more we cleared out the more rolled in, and we were kept quite busy keeping the trench fit for use should we have to use it.

Each outpost kept in communication during the daytime by helio-graph and during the night by patrols. These patrols were much more pleasant than those in Flanders. A patrol of about five men and one NCO would set out from our outpost until it came into contact with a patrol from another outpost. Greetings and passwords were exchanged, a chat and a smoke, and then each patrol returned to its own company. Through the whole night this procedure continued, thus keeping watch that no enemy passed between the outposts.

During the day scouts mounted on horses went out to the front about four miles. Camel scouts also went out into the desert about seven miles, these scouts' young camels being able to travel much faster and farther over the loose sand. Very often these scouts returned dragging along with them, tied to a rope secured to the saddle, a desert Bedouin. These desert tramps were mostly found to be spies for the Turks, and after a thorough interrogation they were usually taken out a little way in the desert and shot.

Aeroplanes went out and watched the movements of the Turks,

reporting them hundreds of miles away. Away in the distance could be seen the faint outline of a range of hills. Johnny Turk was somewhere behind these hills and was reluctant to cross the desert during the dry season, which was close at hand. Patiently we waited for him to come and make his attack, but we waited in vain, and the Command in Eygpt must have thought also that this kind of warfare was too easy for us, for once again we were ordered to pack up ready to move. Tents were struck, blankets rolled into bundles of ten and stacked along with the cooking utensils ready to be loaded on to the backs of the camels, which had been busy during our stay in the desert in bringing up daily our rations and water. Five of these camels and their native drivers came along to our company to take our camp equipment to the railhead. The company moved off, and I and the two old cooks were detailed off to accompany and take charge of the company's luggage. I did not know a word of these native drivers' language so I motioned to them to get their camels down ready for loading up. Four of the natives got their camels down, but the fifth native, who was the leader, left his camel standing and made me understand that his young camel did not carry anything except him. Anyhow, we soon had the tents, blankets and dixies loaded on the camels, and here I learned the meaning of the old saying 'A straw can break a camel's back'. I was also very surprised at the big load a camel can carry quite easily, mile after mile across the arid desert.

Soon our little caravan moved off to the railhead, the leader of the natives walking beside his camel which was in the lead, the others following on in single file, I and the two cooks struggling and perspiring under our heavy packs and rifles alongside, and during the hottest part of the day. As the sun blazed down on us I decided to light a fag and have a smoke, and hooking my thumbs under my shoulder strap I pulled away at the cigarette. The native leader was walking alongside me now; suddenly, like a flash of lightning, he snatched the fag from my mouth and ran on ahead about a hundred yards, turning and grinning at me and triumphantly puffing away at my cigarette. For a moment I gazed at the grinning native and one of the cooks who had seen his action uttered a curse. Then I knelt down on one knee, sighted my rifle and pulled the trigger, sending a bullet whistling within a few inches of his head. He came back to us in leaps and bounds, falling on the sand at my feet, offering me back my cigarette and begging for mercy. One of the cooks added to his terror by drawing a bayonet and placing the point of it against the man's chest.

Of course the little cavalcade had halted while this scene was being enacted in the desert. The other natives grinned and seemed quite pleased to see their leader snivelling in the sand for mercy. With a few swear words and a good kick to help him on his way, we motioned to him to get up and get a move on to the railhead. Needless to say I had no

82

further use for a half cigarette that had been in his dirty mouth and lay still burning on the sand, and picking it up I threw it to him. Eagerly he caught it and placed it between his lips, then suddenly he brought his camel to a halt and, getting it down on the sand, he invited me, by motions, to ride it.

I knew that this offer was a great honour to me, as these young camels are almost sacred to these natives. Anyhow, I preferred third-class riding to walking, and accepted the invitation. With the help of the two cooks and the native I managed to mount with my heavy pack on my back and my rifle slung. Up I rose into the air, taking good care that I did not fall off, and then I swung along, one long stride throwing me on to the front of the wooden saddle and the next stride throwing me back again. This was my first ride on a camel and I cannot say that I enjoyed it, but as I looked down on to the two old cooks sweating and struggling along in the loose sand, the hot mid-day sun beating down on them, for once I preferred the hump.

When we reached the railhead and caught up with the company my sergeant-major saw us arrive and came over to us. Seeing me mounted up on the camel he asked how long I had been in the Camel Corps, and then bursting out into real sergeant-major language he asked me what I thought of myself riding while the two old cooks, old enough to be my father, had to struggle alongside. Of course my sergeant-major had a fine command and was a great soldier when the enemy was hundreds of miles away, but a little explanation by one of the cooks soon enlightened him, and the subject was changed.

Quickly everything was loaded up on the wagons, and with the boys seated on top of tents and equipment, we were pulled by the little steam engine the few miles back to the Suez Canal, which we again crossed, and marched back to our original camp outside Suez. We did not stay here long this time, and after two weeks of parading and visiting the town of Suez in the evenings we packed up once more, handed the camp to Indian soldiers and marched off to Port Tewfik.

Here, at the eastern end of the canal, a steamer was waiting to take us aboard. As to where she was to sail to we were, as usual, ignorant. Rumour said Salonika, Mesopotamia, France and England for a short leave, but as usual Tommy went aboard like a lamb, not knowing whether it was to the pasture or to the slaughter. Anyhow, once aboard we didn't worry much about the morrow and set about making ourselves comfortable for the sail, to wherever it may be.

She was a very decent boat and our quarters and food were excellent. We had not been aboard many hours when she began to move, turning her nose for the entrance to the canal. It was about five o'clock in the evening when we slowly entered the canal. The sailors informed us that we should emerge at the other end at about five o'clock in the morning, the passage through the canal usually taking about twelve hours.

It was rather strange, I could hardly believe that I was on board a big liner as we sailed slowly along that 99-mile-long waterway. The sandy desert stretched for hundreds of miles on either side of us. English troops stationed by the canal ran alongside the ship, enquiring what mob we were and whether certain friends were aboard, actually holding a conversation with us as we leaned over the deck rail. A decent jump from the deck would have landed one clean on the bank.

In places lovely vegetation grew on the banks and at intervals where the canal widened we saw the sand dredgers which kept the waterway navigable. There was a lot I could not see because night came on, darkness settled on the desert, and we went below to play cards, perhaps have a little tale telling and singing, and then sleep while our ship kept up its steady eight miles per hour, sailing through the desert.

When I awoke next morning I learned that we were out of the canal and anchored at Port Said. I ran on deck and looked across a few hundred yards of water at this famous port. Looking further along down a rough breakwater running out to sea, I could see the high statue of de Lesseps, the engineer who cut the Suez Canal. We learned from the crew that our ship was to be coaled here and would stay probably twenty-four hours. I longed to go ashore and have a look round, and my opportunity came later in the morning when the general on board gave permission for all officers and NCOs to go ashore for four hours. I and three other NCOs took advantage of this offer and for threepence each an Egyptian rowed us ashore in his little boat.

We spent our time seeing what we could of Port Said in the time available – not forgetting a good feed and drink. We bought a few small presents for relatives and friends at home, views and souvenirs of the place, and we exchanged English coins for Egyptian and Turkish ones with the wily native who paraded the street showing his collection in a glass case which he pushed about like a perambulator. I managed to complete my set of Turkish coins with one of these fellows and then it was time to be getting back to the ship, all of us being glad to have set foot in Port Said.

When we got back on deck a number of coal barges came alongside loaded almost to sinking point. Scores of natives with wicker baskets and dressed in the most comical and varied fashion imaginable sat on top of the coal. Wooden planks were soon fixed across from the barges to the bunkers of our ship and while some of the natives remained on the barges filling the baskets with coal others ran up the planks in a continual stream, carrying the baskets of coal on their heads or shoulders, emptying the coal in the bunkers and then running down the plank again, screaming and acting just like little boys and girls, jumping from the plank onto the coal in their bare feet just as if it was a soft carpet they were dropping on to. As they passed us they grinned or pulled a funny face, at the same time uttering something utterly unintelligible at us. Should one of them try to shirk his work a fist or a foot from one of the native bosses sent the idler sprawling into the sea, but before one could say Jack Robinson he was in the barge again and dashing up the plank with his basket on his head, smiling broadly as if the whole thing was a good joke.

That night we had another good, sound sleep but were awakened early. The ship was on her way again now and orders were coming round. The lifebelt had to be one's constant companion and we were detailed off to our lifeboat stations, where we had to run immediately on hearing the alarm sounded on the ship's siren. Apart from the danger of torpedoes, life on the ship was very easy and pleasant, the only parade being half an hour's physical training each morning. The food was excellent and plentiful, the divisional band was aboard and through the courtesy of our general gave us a musical treat every afternoon, and everybody was surprised during the evening concert at the talented artistes we had on the ship.

The sail had been quite uneventful so far. We had sailed on by Malta, not calling at the island, and soon we were passing the toe of Italy and on by the island of Sicily. Here was to be our first exciting incident. It was Sunday morning and we had just had divine service on deck, the band having played the hymns for us. A number of the boys had just gone below to help prepare for dinner and others were lounging about the deck. Suddenly the ship's gun aft, manned by naval gunners, boomed out and a shell screeched across the water, followed in a few moments by another. The alarm sounded and we dashed to our positions by the lifeboats. The ship turned suddenly and went full speed ahead and as we waited for further orders we almost expected the terrific explosion of a torpedo.

The voice of a naval officer on the bridge called out, 'Calm down, boys, the danger is past.' Quickly recovering from the sudden shock, we dashed to the rear of the ship and away in the distance we could see the conning tower and periscope of a submarine. It appeared that the U boat had suddenly appeared from behind a small island and given chase to our ship, but she discovered that we were too fast for her and had turned tail again when she found the chase hopeless. The alert gunners of ours had spotted her and let her have a couple of rounds, just to show her that we were quite aware of her presence. The crew afterwards told us that our ship was very fast and her speed had saved us.

Nothing exciting happened during the remainder of the sail and soon we came in sight of a rocky coastline. We sailed along this coast for a few hours and then found ourselves just outside a lovely harbour. It was a grand sight from the deck of our ship. The sea around us was an emerald green that spread out to the tall, rocky cliffs towering on either side of us. On top of the cliffs, shining in the sunlight, were the white walls of a great fort. Looking straight ahead, over the bow of the ship, was a great city, her white buildings stretching from the hills around down to the water's edge, while in the docks and anchored out in the harbour were scores of ships of all sorts and sizes, and belonging to almost every country.

5

The Somme and Blighty

The 1st Battalion the Lancashire Fusiliers, commanded by Lieutenant-Colonel M. Magniac, reached Marseilles aboard SS *Militiades* in March 1916. The 29th Division, of which it continued to form part, went into the line near Beaumont Hamel on the Somme sector, at the time a relatively quiet part of the Western Front, Magniac, a capable and aggressive commander, soon to be awarded the DSO, embarked upon a vigorous policy of raiding, and on the night of 3-4 June the battalion mounted its first raid in France. Other raids followed, and Ashurst was involved in several of them.

We were sailing into Marseilles, the French Mediterranean port, and here we were to disembark and make our way up north, to help the boys engaged on that terrible front the Somme. We spent our first night in this port on board and next day I was put in charge of a few men, to transfer the battalion's kit from the boat to the train. This gave me a chance to have a very hurries look at Marseilles. I think people of every nationality could be seen in the port, and from what little I did see, and what a couple of hospital orderlies who worked in a hospital there told me, it was a very gay and immoral place. Anyhow, we had little time to look round for ourselves as that same evening we entrained.

We were packed as usual in the cattle-trucks for the long ride in front of us. We were issued with enough tea and sugar, biscuits and bully beef to last the journey. During the daytime we opened wide the sliding doors of the truck and sat with our legs dangling out as we admired the lovely country and villages we passed during that long trip through the heart of France.

It was springtime now, and after staring at the sandy desert for months the sight of lovely trees and gardens and green grass was good to our eyes. Now and again the train stopped and backed into a siding for convenience. During these halts there was a general dash up to the engine for hot water to brew tea, the engine driver swearing at us in French, afraid we would empty his tender. The villagers also made hay while the sun shone, selling to the troops bread, cakes, chocolates, etc. Huge tubs of water were also provided at these halts for the troops' toilet, and the boys needed this wash badly as on the journey they had procured old buckets or tins which were quickly made into braziers, and in the cool of the evenings fires were made in them with wood from the ration boxes and coal, again from the engine. The braziers were hung out of the truck, swinging in the breeze, until most of the smoke had cleared away and the speed of the train had fanned the fire into a bright glare. The troop train looked quite weird as it sped along in the darkness with the braziers hanging out from the trucks and blazing brightly.

Then, when the fire was nice and bright, it was drawn inside the truck, the doors were closed, and as the old cattle-trucks rattled along we told yarns or settled down to a very disturbed and uncomfortable sleep, awakening with a black face and an awfully dry throat from the fumes. After three nights and two days of jolting along like this a bugle call rang out along the train. This was the usual signal that we had only a few more miles to go. Each man began to sort out his own rifle and equipment and prepare them for the road. Soon our train slowed down and drew into the little village of Pont Rémy. The officers came along from their cosy compartments with the usual 'jump to it' orders. Quickly we formed into platoons and fours and moved off.

We were really glad of the march after our long ride, for our bones were sore and limbs stiff. Nine miles we marched, to another village where we rested for the night in barns, the straw feeling nice and soft after the hard floor of the cattle-trucks. Next morning we moved on again to another village, where we again settled down in barns, remaining at this village for three days, and being able to buy bread, eggs and milk from the villagers, and sleeping on a soft bed of straw in a comfortable barn. We soon felt fit and well and acclimatised.

After our rest we moved on, nearer and nearer to the dreaded firing line, eventually arriving at Achieu Wood, a large wood right behind the Somme front. Tents and wooden huts were our homes in this wood for two weeks. When it rained it was ankle-deep in mud, and we had to keep the drains deep and clean around the huts to keep us from being flooded out. Trenches were dug in the wood for shelter in case of air raids by Fritz, who very often came over at a great height and dropped his bombs on the wood.

Now the serious work of training began and we had stiff parades and night operations to fit us for the line. It was here in Achieu Wood that we were first issued with the steel helmet. The boys did not like the idea of wearing this heavy headgear, but Headquarters made it known that to be caught not wearing one in the trenches constituted a crime.

One day a few officers and men from each company were issued with new maps and marched off out of the camp. We knew quite well what their mission was: they were going to look over the section of the line we were going to take over. During the next two days our kit was inspected, deficiences were made up, new field bandages were issued, rifles were well cleaned and oiled, and after tea we moved off up the line. It was a long march, first along the roads and then across the open fields, and finally down the long communication trenches. Shells came over but dropped hundreds of yards away from us and we reached the front line without a casualty.

The particular part of the front we took over was called 'White City' by the boys. They gave it this name from the great heaps of white chalk lying about which had been shovelled out of the earth during the making of the deep dug-outs in the reserve trenches. In front of us and in the German lines were the remains of what was once a pretty village, Beaumont Hamel. Even its very foundations were now torn from the earth by our great howitzer shells. Our engineers were also tunnelling slowly forward, deep down in the earth towards the village, to wipe it clean off the face of the earth with one mighty blow at the given signal.

It was spring now and weather conditions in the line were not too bad, but it was a hot shop, Fritz being keenly on the alert and shelling us regularly and heavily, sending over the dreaded Minenwefers, the great trench mortars that we could see falling out of the sky towards us like great black chunks of death.

Our period of duty on this front was ten days at a stretch, and when relief came lots of men were not equal to the task of walking back the seven or eight miles to the rest village. We struggled along round the traverse of the communication trench tired, dirty, unshaven, lurching against the clay sides like drunken men, the heavy steel helmets weighing down on heads that had not known a peaceful sleep for ten days, and holding the memory of the last agonising moments of a good pal. Was it any wonder that men collapsed, their foreheads were bathed, and they rested awhile, then a pal just a mite stronger helped them on their way?

On reaching the road far behind the trenches the surface seemed hard and cruel to our tender feet which had been encased in heavy army boots for ten days, and had walked only on the mud or soft clay bottom of a trench. We had left the front line in the darkness of night, but daylight had broken now and a spring morning was round about us. We stopped to rest a while, sitting or half lying about on the grassy bank beside the road, drawing in the sweet morning air in between puffs at the comforting old fag. I felt as a man must feel when he steps outside a prison gate after doing a long term of imprisonment. Lumps of dried clay stuck to my clothes and hair, my body itched and felt sore, and ached from the weight of equipment and ammunition that had hung from it for days and nights together, but my heart felt lighter as we moved on again to the cosy barn which would at least shelter us from the rain, and where we could sleep almost peacefully for a whole night. It was a great relief to reach the village of Mailly Maillet and throw down our heavy equipment and rifles and headgear on to the floor of the barn.

Volunteers were soon off for the blankets and rations, and a couple of the boys slipped round to the cookhouse for our bacon and tea, which had been prepared for us by the cooks who had come on ahead of us out of the line. After breakfast we settled down for a few hours' sound sleep, then we set about washing, shaving, scraping and brushing, to make ourselves presentable again. The old stew was dished out and then we set off to explore the village, to find estaminets, canteens or houses where *pommes-de-terre*, *oeufs* and coffee could be bought.

A few days of decent meals, clean underclothes and sound sleep and the bodily weariness of trench life soon wore off, but not so the remembrance of its torture. The day of our return to the trenches was dreaded by most men, and during our recreation and games of football men fervently hoped that their legs would be broken, and actually risked seriously crippling themselves in order to gain admission to hospital, and even in their calmer moments deliberately devised the means to get dysentery or blood poisoning. A few more desperate men deserted, only to be caught again and shot for cowardice. Like all the rests out of the line, it seemed much shorter than the same period in the line, and once again we were making our way to White City.

In the dusk of the evening we moved quickly down the long communication trenches, pushing past the orderlies and cooks who were coming out of the line as the advance party of the battalion we were about to relieve. Odd bullets began to ping over our heads and Fritz's whiz-bangs burst on either side of the trench, but we passed by the reserve trenches and into the front line safely, taking over our part of the trench from the boys who were holding it, and who quickly and quietly slipped off with a parting goodnight and 'Good luck, lads.'

Sentries were posted and the usual nightly stunts commenced. Men were detailed off on wiring parties, slipping over the top with bundles of iron stakes on their shoulders, others struggling with heavy drums of barbed wire. Quickly and silently these men worked, hardly daring to breathe as they screwed the stakes down into the ground and ran the barbed wire crosswise from stake to stake, suddenly standing still, not daring to make the slightest move as Fritz sent a star light flaring in the sky, lighting up no-man's-land. Then at intervals, as if suspecting what we were doing, Fritz would spray our wire with machine-gun bullets, often catching the boys unaware with these sudden bursts and killing and wounding many of them.

Patrols were usually sent out into no-man's-land to protect these working parties from any German patrols that may be prowling about. One night I was given orders to take three men along with me, cut a path through our barbed wire and proceed along no-man's-land to my right, where I had to come in and report to the Dublin Fusiliers. Of course the Dubs' sentries were warned of my patrol out in front and were given the password, which I had selected myself, using the name of my native town, Wigan.

Discarding our steel helmets and placing woollen comforters on our heads, we placed a couple of bombs in our pockets and, buckling on a revolver, I jumped quickly on top of the trench, gripping a heavy pair of wire clippers. The men who were going with me were fairly new out to the front and had not patrolled before. Anyhow, I lay flat beneath our wire and called for the others to follow, but just as the first man got his body half out of the trench Fritz opened fire with a machine gun, sending a hail of bullets whistling about a foot above my prone body. Back into the trench dropped the first man of my patrol, but as the firing ceased I called softly again to them to have another try.

Eventually, thanks to the silence of Fritz's gun, I managed to get them on top of the trench, and whispering to them to follow me in single file I crawled along on my back, reaching up with my clippers and quickly cutting the strands of wire, moving alternately from left to right so that when the breach in the wire was made it would not be noticeable to the enemy. Several times during this operation Fritz's gun burst out, or a star light shone brightly for a few moments, causing us to cling to the ground and lie like logs of wood.

Having cut through the wire, we crawled together and held a whispered conversation. Warning my men to have bombs ready and make the least possible sound, I moved on, the others keeping in close touch with me, stopping now and again to listen for the sound of an enemy patrol and ready instantly to hurl a bomb in their direction. Happily, however, we met no Germans prowling about and watching keenly the landmarks as a star light flared up, I made my way towards the Dubs' trenches, hearing the hard breathing of my comrades behind me as we slowly advanced. Approaching the Dubs' wire carefully, I could faintly see a sentry's head above the parapet. Softly I called to him, 'Hello, Dubs.' His rifle was thrust quickly forward and I dropped flat, but instead of pulling the trigger he called softly and eagerly, 'Is that you, Wigan?' Receiving an answer in the affirmative, he called out, 'Move a little to your left and you will find an opening in the wire.' Quickly I found the opening and with a sigh of relief we dropped down into the Dubs' trench. I reported to the officer in charge and then our little patrol made its way back to our own front line, marking the spot where I had cut the wire by driving a wooden stake into the trench right opposite the opening.

On reporting to my company officer he allowed us a tot of rum and excused us further duty for the remainder of the night. We retired to our six-foot-deep dug-out and tried to settle down for an hour's sleep until dawn, but the rats with which the place was infested continually ran over our bodies, sometimes cheekily sitting on us until with a curse and a violent shake the rodents were sent flying across the dug-out.

Raids and patrolling in no-man's-land were nightly occurrences by now and the sector we held was becoming a warm place indeed. Just over half-way from our trench to the German trench in no-man's-land was a sunken road running parallel with the front lines. Almost every night there was a miniature battle between our patrols and the Germans for possession of this sunken road. Fritz usually got there first because he was nearer to it and consequently had the advantage. Many an officer and man was killed by the bombs these patrols hurled at each other during those scraps in the darkness of night for the sunken road.

Our commanding officer decided that some night we must possess that sunken road at all costs. His little idea was to send out a strong patrol in the night and take the road by force, then for the patrol to remain there until the following night. So one officer, two NCOs and ten men were detailed for this little stunt and I was one of the NCOs. Silently our party proceeded across no-man's-land, a couple of the boys carrying canvas water buckets in which was a good supply of bombs.

As we approached silently near to the road we could hear the faint movements of the Germans. A whisper from our officer in charge passed silently from one to another. It was the order to hurl our bombs into the road and charge the instant he fired his revolver. A few moments later his revolver spat out; instantly our bombs whizzed through the air and at the same time we sprang forward for the sunken road.

Our bombs had hardly exploded as we jumped down in the road, but Fritz had been wide awake and skedaddled back to his own lines. We sent another few bullets and bombs after him in the darkness but didn't know what damage we had done. Soon Fritz sprayed no-man's-land with machine-gun bullets, but we were quite safe from these in the sunken road. Then quickly and quietly we dug little manholes into the side of the road nearest to the enemy, just for cover in case Fritz fell to our little game and decided to shell us out of it.

We had no further trouble that night and daylight came. During that long day we lay in our little dug-outs, munching biscuits and bully beef. We dare not make tea or smoke for our lives. Then as night once again approached we grew a little excited and wondered if Fritz would make his early dash to the sunken road, little dreaming that we had been waiting for him all day. It had hardly gone dark when, sure enough, Fritz was coming quickly, almost silently, about ten or a dozen of them, judging by the faint creeping shadows.

Breathlessly we waited for them and the crack of our officer's pistol which again was the signal to hurl our bombs, which we gripped in our hands, the safety pins already drawn. Fritz was almost at the road when the pistol cracked. We hurled our bombs as fast as we could draw the pins and pumped bullets into them as fast as the triggers of the pistols could be pulled. Fritz certainly got the shock of his life, and with howls of rage and pain quickly made back for his own lines. Groans and shouts told us that our bombs had played havoc with them, but sharply from our officer in charge came the order, 'Back for your lives, boys.' Quickly we scrambled out of the sunken road and ran as fast as possible in the darkness for our front line. Falling into shell-holes, we jumped up and ran on, not feeling the knocks and bruises in that mad dash for the safety of our front line. Fritz was beginning to light up no-man's-land now with his star lights and we knew that any moment he would rake our wire with machine guns. Reaching our barbed wire, we dashed through the zigzag opening, tearing our clothes and also our flesh on the barbs, then jumped into the trench to lie exhausted awhile as Fritz played tunes on our wire with his bullets. That little stunt was hailed as a success, only two of our party being wounded and all of them getting back to our lines.

During the daytime Fritz did his best to dishearten us by sticking up boards out of his trenches on which was written, in English, bad news such as 'A great defeat on the Ypres sector; thousands of Tommies taken prisoner' or news that we had lost a great naval battle and half our navy had gone to the bottom on the sea. Of course we did not believe any of his lies and we were forbidden to write anything at all on boards for Fritz's information. But one day during ration issue a corporal of ours stuck up a loaf of bread on the end of a bayonet and raised it high for Fritz to see. Almost instantly two bayonets with loaves of bread on them were thrust up out of the German line.

I think that rats also infested White City in battalions. Whether it was the chalk trenches or the numerous dead bodies buried there that attracted them I don't know, for they were quite at home and even had the manners to stand aside while you passed them in the trenches, and they looked quite offended if you kicked at them. Some of the boys swore that the rodents carried tin openers with them for food was only safe when it was carried on the person.

Sometimes we indulged in a little amusement, and at the same time helped to lessen the activities of these four-footed thieves. Placing a piece of cheese about three inches from a rat hole we waited patiently, rifle at the ready and finger on trigger, for the lightning dash we knew the rat would make before long. Soon a little twitching, whiskered nose would protrude from the hole; the army cheese would be too tempting a morsel to miss. Out would shoot half the rat's body, and as quickly the finger would press the trigger, bang, and Mr Rodent's body would be flung over the back of the trench, almost in two halves.

When not on sentry duty or patrolling or wiring in no-man's-land, working parties always kept one well awake. I hardly know which of these dangerous nightly jobs was the worst – crawling about no-man's-land on one's stomach, or carrying up from the rear great 'football' bombs and 'flying pigs' to the trench mortar emplacements, or, with rifle slung and a heavy box of ammunition on one's shoulder, slipping and sliding along the muddy trenches, the sharp edges of the heavy box almost cutting into your collar bone, and, when a whiz-bang screamed at you, dropping the box with a thud and cowering down to the bottom of the trench. Being detailed for the ration party meant a long trek behind, to return carrying a sandbag full of bread, struggling gallantly to keep it dry for it was all that your comrades would get for the next twenty-four hours, and, if given the sandbag that contained the big stone bottle of rum, taking extra precautions that a stray bullet or piece of shell didn't break it and spill the precious stuff – a loss that was altogether unforgivable by the boys.

As each day went by this Beaumont Hamel front became hotter and hotter; our artillery were very active and Fritz sent over more stuff in reply, causing a lot of casualties amongst the boys. Information about the enemy in front of us was wanted by our command in rear, so raids to get this information were the order. These bombing raids were very dangerous expeditions and nearly always resulted in heavy casualties. These bombing parties usually comprised about thirty officers and men. The raids were made in conjunction with the artillery; times were stated, watches synchronised, and when darkness came everything was prepared and ready and the raid began. Our faces were blacked and everything that might jingle was securely fastened about the body, then over the top we went, creeping quickly and silently over to Fritz's barbed wire, under which we would slip a long Bangalore torpedo, setting it ready to fire at a moment's notice.

We could hear the German sentries talking to each other in the trench, and as they fired a star light into the air we would lie as still as corpses. We waited with hearts thumping for the vital moment. Suddenly pandemonium broke loose, our artillery firing rapidly and putting a box barrage onto the particular part of Fritz's line that we were to raid. Shells would scream close over our heads and the German front line seemed literally alive with explosions and flying dirt. The din was terrific and odd shells fell dangerously near to us. For two long minutes this fierce bombardment would go on, then all at once the barrage would lift onto Fritz's reserve trenches.

This was the moment for us to move, and move very quickly. Bang went the torpedo and up went a portion of Fritz's wire entanglements; then a quick rush through the breach into Fritz's front line, to capture any German who might be still alive. A bomb or a bullet soon settled any that might have shown fight, then quickly back into no-man's-land again with our captives. All this was done in a few minutes' time before our artillery again dropped the barrage on to Fritz's front line.

By now Fritz would have got over the shock; his artillery would be quickly retaliating and his machine guns sweeping the darkness. It was every man for himself now and often we lost our prisoners, their own guns killing them in that wild dash to safety. On reaching our trenches we reported to headquarters, and carried on at the normal duty of sentry or bombing post.

After a raid such as this we knew what to expect from Fritz, and sure enough he would bombard our trenches with both light and heavy shells, often doing great damage and wounding lots of men. Then up would go our SOS to our artillery, who soon gave Fritz his change, which usually settled matters for a while.

General Sir Douglas Haig had taken over from Field-Marshal Sir John French as commander of the British army in France and Belgium on 19 December 1915. He was immediately involved in delicate negotiations with the French over plans for a forthcoming Allied offensive, and in February it was agreed that the British would collaborate in a major offensive on the Somme. But the German offensive at Verdun, launched in February 1916, swallowed up French reserves which were to have been used on the Somme, and, in the event, the British were to play the major part in the battle.

The main blow was to be struck by Lieutenant-General Sir Henry Rawlinson's Fourth Army, which held a twenty-mile front between Maricourt in the south and Hebuterne in the north. General Sir Edmund Allenby's Third Army was to mount a diversionary attack at Gommecourt, further to the north. Over most of this front, and particularly towards the south, terrain favoured the Germans. Their trenches, solidly dug into the chalk uplands during the time that the Somme was a quiet sector, linked fortified villages like Montauban, Fricourt and Thiepval. Redoubts secured ground not dominated by villages, and positions were carefully sited so as to bring flanking fire onto attackers making their way up the dog's tooth row of spurs and re-entrants.

A crushing bombardment was the crucial ingredient of the British plan. Between 24 June and zero hour on the morning of 1 July, 1,508,652 shells were fired – more than in the first year of the war. On the heels of the bombardment Rawlinson's infantry, the bulk of them New Army battalions, raised in 1914 as a response to Lord Kitchener's appeal for troops, were to advance to occupy the ground devastated by the gunners. Lieutenant-General Sir Hubert Gough's Reserve Army (soon renamed the Fifth Army) would press through the gap thus ripped in the German lines. The attack was widely believed to be the 'big push' which would end the war, and preparations were detailed and elaborate.

One night in early June we left the trenches for a rest that lasted about three weeks, and during this rest we learned, and were quite satisfied, that a big push was about to be made in the near future. Great gun emplacements were made and motor lorries brought up great stocks of ammunition which was buried in long trenches. More troops were billeted in the camps and villages just behind the line. Our battalion was made up into full fighting strength and we started intensified training. Each day we practised advancing and attacking.

The village of Beaumont Hamel and the German front line, along with their reserve trenches, were mapped out with white tape in the fields outside our rest village. Every NCO and man was made to thoroughly understand what he had to do when the real advance began. Generals and their staff came to watch us do these manoeuvres and complimented us on the way we did them.

One day the corps commander came to see us and speak to us.[25] The battalion was formed into three sides of a square, and into the centre of it rode the commander followed by our colonel and adjutant and the long trail of staff who usually tail on behind an officer of such high rank. After the usual salutes we received orders to stand at ease and as his horse pranced about our commander began to speak, raising his voice so that all could hear.

He told us of the coming great advance, an advance, he said, that might mean the end of the war. Nothing was being left undone to make it a great success. To give us an idea of the number of guns that would take part in the bombardment, he said that if they were placed side by side – that is, wheel to wheel – they would stretch from the English Channel to the Alps. These guns, both large and small, would shell the German positions until they were flat, and not a German soldier would be left in them to bar our progress. He spoke on about the traditions of our battalion; he knew that he could trust us to do our duty and cover ourselves in glory, as we had already done in the Dardanelles. Then he wished us goodbye and good luck and rode off to tell our neighbouring battalion the same story. I wonder if while he was talking he heard the ugly murmurings in the ranks or noticed our officers turning round and in an undertone order silence and issue threats. Had he heard the remarks of the men when they were dismissed off parade, he would have thought they were not so enthusiastic about the big push.

However, the day of the great advance came nearer. It was decided that one company only of the battalion should hold the line during the week of the bombardment. My own company was detailed for this job and on the day before the big noise started we set off for the front line. We were loaded like mules with rations and ammunition. It was a long journey and as we passed through a cornfield a terrible thunderstorm broke on us. There was no shelter near and quickly we fastened our ground sheets like capes around our shoulders. The rain pelted down on us in torrents, the lightning danced around us and the thunder was deafening. Still on we went, splashing through the pools, hearing a curse as some chap slipped and went sprawling with his heavy load. Weighing down also on our minds was the thought that any one of us would be lucky to return alive from the terrible battle that was before us. No wonder that we longed for a shell to come and give us a Blighty.

Eventually, wet through and fed up we reached the wood at Auchonvillers and dropped into the long communication trench that led to the front line. As we walked around its numerous curves and bends in single file the thick herbage and wild flowers hung over the sides of the trench and brushed our faces, splashing us with fresh raindrops.

Suddenly from out of the sky a shell came screaming at us. Down we dropped to the bottom of the trench, but the shell might have had eyes to see us – right over our heads it burst, one of Fritz's high explosive shrapnel shells. The nose cap hummed and hit the floor with a thud and the iron balls the shell was loaded with pit-patted all about us. I heard a sudden shout of pain and knew at once that one of the boys had got it. Word soon passed from one to another that so-and-so had got it in the shoulder and so-and-so in the hand. Of course the two boys soon had their wounds dressed and were quickly making their way back again to the nearest dressing station, while we moved on, secretly envying our two comrades their pain.

We passed the reserve trenches and reached the front line without further casualties, relieving the battalion there who, wishing us luck, soon showed us their heels.

During the 'big bang' it would only be necessary for a look-out to be in the front line, and after the look-out had been told off the remainder began to settle down in the deep dug-outs to make themselves as comfortable as possible until it was time to spring over the top a week hence.

Next day the fun began. What a terrible noise! Guns of all kinds and sizes were firing rapidly; the din of hundreds of shells whizzing over our heads was like several ghostlike express trains hurtling through the sky. One could hardly hear the remarks of a chum outside in the trench, and in the dug-out one felt the thud of the great shells as they dropped down on to Fritz's trenches, churning them up again and again amidst a cloud of flame and smoke and dust.

Fritz kept strangely quiet, just sending over a few long-distance shells that did little or no damage. He knew that later on he would need every bit of ammunition and patiently reserved his fire. The greatest danger to us was when our own big shells fell short and almost blew in our dug-outs. For a few hours each day the guns seemed to cool down a while, only to burst out again in full fury. What a spectacle it was to stand quite upright in our front line at night time, looking back to see the sky illuminated with hundreds of large and small flashes like lightning dancing on the distant ridges, and listening to the continuous roar of big and little shells passing overhead, then to turn about and look towards Fritz's lines, to see a sight that made one feel pity even for an enemy.

His front-line trenches could be plainly seen in the light of continuously bursting shells, broken and replaced by great craters; his barbed wire entanglements were blown into a knotted and twisted mass. Pieces of wood and wire, fragments of sandbags and lumps of mother earth continually rose and fell in the thick powder smoke. Great howitzer shells dug deep into his line before they exploded, shaking the very ground under our feet four or five hundred yards away, lifting tons of debris into the air and leaving a gaping hole in which a house could be placed.

One night above the noise of the flying shells and explosions we heard the roar of an aeroplane engine and there at a great height was an illuminated aeroplane. The usual red, white and blue rings under each wing were lit up. It was the first illuminated aeroplane I had seen in my life. What its mission was I do not know and never heard, but it had no sooner appeared over the line than it disappeared, never to be seen again by us during that bombardment.[26]

During the daytime we played cards in the dug-out, getting quite used to awful din. It was while having a game of cards one day that we were requested to go out into the trench and be photographed, presumably just fixing bayonets ready to go over the top. It was only a few minutes of a job and we soon obliged, especially as the photographer or war correspondent, or whatever he was, promised us a tot of rum and a packet of cigarettes for our trouble. Anyhow, it certainly was the last photo a lot of those gallant lads ever had taken. [27]

On the last night in June, after a week living under that terrible racket, hundreds of men in full fighting kit, and strangely quiet, came streaming down the trenches, packing the front line and reserve trenches. Lots of them had picks or shovels pushed through their equipment straps, and others carried short trench ladders, their haversacks bulging out with iron rations, even bombs, and water bottles filled to overflowing.

Trench-mortar crews, struggling along carrying the heavy parts of their guns, artillery observers, signallers and RAMC men with the white armlet on which was a plain red cross, and carrying large-size water bottles and stretchers, were all making their way to their allotted places. By dawn the trenches were crowded with men and it was almost difficult to move about.

The 29th Division was to assault Beaumont Hamel, a fortified village above the Ancre, its front dominated by the spurs of Redan Ridge and Hawthorn Ridge, and protected by wire which patrols had already discovered to have been scarcely touched by the bombardment. The 86th Brigade, of which the Lancashire Fusiliers formed part, had the German first line, including Beaumont Hamel itself, as its objective.

The high ground of Hawthorn Ridge, to the battalion's right front, was dominated by the Hawthorn Redoubt. Beneath it the Royal Engineers had placed a mine containing 45,000 pounds of ammonal. There was considerable debate over the time at which this should be detonated, and it was eventually decided to blow it at 7.20, ten minutes before zero hour. This decision has been described as 'a fatal error'. Not only did it give the Germans immediate warning of the attack but it also led to both the divisional and corps artillery plans being modified so that at the moment of the assault much of the available artillery would have switched from the forward trenches.

Between the trenches held by the Lancashire Fusiliers and the German first line, about 350 yards away, ran a sunken road between ten and fifteen feet deep, the scene of several patrol actions over the previous weeks. In the early hours of 1 July, B and D companies moved across no-man's-land and occupied the sunken road, where they were joined by 100 men of the Brigade Bombing Company and eight Stokes trench mortars. A tunnel and trench, finished that morning, linked the sunken road with the British front line, but orders emphasised that it would be used only by runners and for getting telephone wires and water pipes forward. The mortars were to open a 'hurricane bombardment' on the German front line at 7.20, and ten minutes later the forward companies were to assault while the two rear companies crossed no-man's-land to support them.

We had all received our special instructions and been informed that the huge mine under Beaumont Hamel which the Sappers had been preparing for weeks would be blown up at 7.30 a.m., and the great explosion would be the signal to go over the top. We had all received a stiff tot of rum and some of the officers and NCOs had certainly had a very stiff tot, which was very plain to some of us who did not have access to the stone jar, or carry flasks. I was detailed off in charge of a party of eight bombers and we were supposed to be the colonel's bodyguard. We took up our position in a communication trench leading into the front line. There we stood, rather silently leaning against the side of the trench, wondering if we had much longer to live and suddenly brushing the ugly thought of death away and thinking that a nice Blighty would come to us quickly. As a huge German shrapnel shell burst overhead we came to earth again and openly expressed the view to each other that we might get it sharp, whether it was Blighty or death.

Fritz's guns seemed to be coming to life now; his shells were dropping over pretty merrily and machine-gun bullets whistled over our heads, just as if he knew as well as we did that the time was near. Just as the waiting was becoming unbearable and the terrible strain causing some men to utter almost unnatural noises, we felt a queer dull thud and our trench fairly rocked, and a great blue flame shot into the sky, carrying with it hundreds of tons of bricks and stone and great chunks of earth mingled with wood and wire and fragments of sandbags.

The great mine had gone up. It was 7.30, zero hour. We set our teeth; we seemed to say to ourselves all in a moment, 'To hell with life', and, as the shout of our comrades in the front line leaping over the top reached us above the din of battle, we bent low in the trench and moved forward. Fritz's shells were screaming down on us fast now; huge black shrapnel shells seemed to burst on top of us. Shouts of pain and calls for help could be heard on all sides; as we pushed forward, we stepped over mortally wounded men who tried to grab our legs as we passed them, or we squeezed to one side of the trench while wounded men struggled by us anxious to get gaping wounds dressed and reach the safety of the dug-outs in rear.

Ashurst is wrong in believing that the mine went up at 7.30: it was blown, as planned, at 7.20. But he may be forgiven for minor slips in his recollection of what passed on that bright, bloody morning, for things had already begun to go wrong even before the mine exploded. At about 7.00 the Germans noticed the new trench leading into the sunken road and shelled the road with 77mm field guns, causing 20 casualties. At 7.30 the leading sections of B and D Companies 'dashed forward in extended order', as the battalion's War Diary put it. They had a few moments' grace before German machine-gunners opened fire, and the third and fourth lines of the two forward companies were 'practically wiped out within a few yards of the Sunken Road'. To the left rear, A Company suffered severely in its advance to the sunken road; all three platoon commanders were hit. C Company, the right rear company, lost its company commander and CSM as they stood on the parapet giving orders to advance. Second Lieutenant W. R. B. Caseby and about sixty men reached the sunken road, but Lieutenant Jones and his platoon, trying to use the single trench leading to the road, found their way thoroughly blocked by the wounded.

Ashurst and his bombers, who seem to have been left behind in a communication trench leading to the front line when battalion headquarters had moved up to the sunken road at 7 that morning, had to make their way along the trench, with its jetsam of dead and wounded, to reach the front line. Then they had to cross the open ground already littered with the casualties of A and C Companies before reaching the comparative safety of the sunken road, filled with survivors of the two forward companies, most of them wounded, and the A and C Company men who had managed to get that far.

In a few minutes the whole atmosphere of the place had taken on a fearful change. One felt like stopping to help a badly wounded comrade but to stop at such a time was to be accused of cowardice. Men uttered terrible curses even as they lay dying from terrible wounds, and others sat at the bottom on the trench shaking and shouting, not wounded but unable to bear the noise, the smell and the horrible sights.

When we reached the front line trench there was no need to climb out on top. It was already battered flat and our wire entanglements blown to fragments. Instantly I jumped on top and ran as fast as I could through the powder smoke towards the sunken road, two-thirds of the way across no-man's-land, holding down my head as I ran to shield my face as much as possible with my tin hat. The bullets made a horrible hissing noise all round me; shrapnel shells seemed to rend the sky and huge shells screamed down on us, shaking the ground under my feet and blowing to pieces both dead and wounded men who were lying about. Even in that mad dash I could plainly hear the sickly thud as a bullet struck some comrade close by me, and every moment I fully expected a bullet to tear through my body.

Miraculously, I breathlessly reached the sunken road, practically leaping the last yard or two and almost diving into its shelter. Picking myself up and looking round, my God, what a sight! The whole of the road was strewn with dead and dying men. Some were talking deliriously, others calling for help and asking for water.

Some other fit men like myself were bandaging wounded comrades or holding a water bottle to some poor fellow's lips. As the thumping of my heart steadied down a bit and my breathing eased I heard a faint voice quite close to me calling 'Corporal'. There I recognised one of my boys, his face deathly pale and his tunic saturated in blood. Quickly I held my water bottle to his lips. He drank just a little and then as he smiled up at me I heard the colonel calling out for all fit men to line the bank of the road, waving his revolver menacingly as he did so. Then he called for a signaller. One stepped up to him. 'Get to the top of that road and signal for reinforcements quickly,' he thundered. Without a moment's hesitation the signaller obeyed, but as he raised his flags to send the first letter the brave fellow dropped back into the road, riddled with bullets. The picture of that gallant hero's brave act will never leave my memory, but no sooner had the signaller's body crashed back into the road than the colonel's voice rang out again – 'Now men, as soon as I give the word over you go again, and this time don't stop until you reach that front line.' Then quickly jumping up out of the road he called at the top of his voice, 'Come on.'

At 8.15 Lieutenant-Colonel Magniac ordered the Stokes mortars in the sunken road to open rapid fire, under cover of which Second Lieutenant Caseby led forward about seventy-five men who had collected in the sunken road. They were caught by machine-gun fire as they crossed the crest-line a few yards in front of the road, and only two officers and ten men reached the German wire. It was probably this attack that Ashurst joined.

Once more we sprang into that fusillade of bullets. In a few moments I must have been alone and quickly decided to drop into a shell-hole. I felt almost certain that most of the men had been killed or wounded. Anyhow, I was quite safe from Fritz's bullets, at least in my shell-hole, and I could look back over no-man's-land towards our own trenches. Hundreds of dead lay about and wounded men were trying to crawl back to safety; their heart rending cries for help could be heard above the noise of rifle fire and bursting shells.

As I lay there watching their painful efforts to get back to our line I noticed these poor fellows suddenly try to rise on their feet and then fall in a heap and lie very still. Surely Fritz wasn't killing these unfortunate men. Shells whistled over my head and dropped amongst the poor fellows, blowing dead men into the air and putting others out of their agony. As I gazed on this awful scene and realised my own terrible danger I asked God to help me. I did not know if the others had reached the German line or not and if Englishmen or Germans were in front of me, and to venture to look might mean certain death.

Now I seemed to have time to think. I suddenly remembered that I had water and was thirsty, and taking my water bottle from its carrier I rolled over on my back and drank. I also thought of the biscuits in my haversack but I was not feeling hungry somehow. I would have loved a smoke but one puff of smoke floating out of my shallow shell-hole might have brought a dozen German bombs in my direction for I was only a few yards from Fritz's line, if he still held it.

Then I began to try and decide my next move. God help me if Fritz

decided to counter-attack; our artillery, in shelling Fritz, would blow me
to bits, and if I escaped that Fritz would find me there, and would he
trouble to take me prisoner or give me a bullet, or, even worse, the
bayonet? If only darkness would come, then I could move, but it was still
only morning on a summer's day and darkness was a long way off.

Over to the right I could see where our neighbouring battalion, The
Royal Fusiliers, had gone over the top. Suddenly I noticed a few of them
running for their lives back to their front line.[28] This made me think that
Fritz was counter-attacking and I fully expected to hear him coming at
the double for my shell-hole. Sudden fear must have spurred me to
action, for in a flash I sprang out of my shell-hole and dashed madly for
the sunken road, flinging myself into it as Fritz's bullets whistled all
about me, and almost jumping on to two of our men who were busy
making a firing step in the side of the road.

Silently congratulating myself on that lucky sprint and feeling
thankful to be out of such a death trap, I walked along the road to find an
officer I could report to. As I picked my way carefully along that terrible
sunken road RAMC men were attending to the wounded and here and
there I recognised some of the boys lying there awfully quiet and still.
The officer was very glad to see me and told me to place myself in charge
of a few men at the bottom end of the road.

The attack launched at 8.15 failed as disastrously as the previous attempt. At 11.45
Brigadier-General Williams of 86th Brigade sent a message saying that he had heard
rumours of a retirement, and ordering Magniac to attack again. Magniac, who had spent
the early part of the battle with his forward troops in the sunken road, and had seen for
himself just how impossible their task was, denied that his men had retired, and
informed Williams that previous attacks had foundered because 'we are mown down by
machine-gun fire and only get a few yards beyond the Sunken Road'. He now had only
one officer and 75 men available for an attack, and considered that any attempt was
bound to fail. It was not until 1.05 that Williams cancelled the order, and by this time
events had shown just how right Magniac was. At 12.30 Major A. T. Le M. Utterson,
who had started the day commanding the 10 per cent battle reserve, deliberately left out
of the first phase of the fighting, left the front line with twenty-five men. He hoped to
collect the survivors in the sunken road and make another attack, but only he and four
men reached the road. During the afternoon the road was prepared for defence, and at
6.00 it was evacuated apart from a party of one officer and twenty men – Ashurst among
them – detailed to stay behind. At about midnight Caseby, two other officers and
twenty men, who had spent the day in a hollow just short of the German wire, joined
them.

Lieutenant-Colonel Magniac had shown physical and moral courage of a high order on
that day, and was fortunate to escape unscathed. He was killed by a shell at Monchy-le-
Preux, near Arras, on 24 April 1917. Ironically, the same shell killed Lieutenant Caseby,
who had been awarded the Military Cross for his gallantry on 1 July 1916.

The battle had considerably died down by now. It was like the calm after
the storm. Fritz had held us and also wiped us out. We busied ourselves
cutting a firing step at the top edge of the road and making ourselves a

little cover in case Fritz decided to try and blow us out of it. We munched the hard biscuits and the bully beef and shared each other's water. And we collected our dead comrades, took off their identity discs, and placed the bodies together tidily. When darkness came at last stretcher bearers came swiftly across the open from our lines, collected the wounded and carried them back to our trenches, totally untroubled by the sniping that Fritz kept up in the darkness.

A messenger also came over from headquarters with a message that one officer, one NCO and twenty men only were to hold the sunken road, all others to retire to our front line. The officer was selected and I was detailed as the NCO. My officer decided to barricade the ends of the road with sandbags, and quickly we got to work.

A party of engineers came across with barbed wire and stakes to put up in front of the road, but Fritz played havoc with the poor fellows, killing and wounding one officer and nine men, and making their task almost impossible. All of the wounded were evacuated from the road during the night and when dawn broke just the officer, myself and the twenty men, along with the dead, were in the road. The officer took charge of the barricade at the top end of the road and I was in charge at the bottom end, seven of the men, with the oldest soldier in charge, taking up a position in the centre of the road.

When daylight came the battlefield was almost quiet, friend and foe seeming to rest after the terrible strain of the day before. I and my half-dozen men were dozing, our rifles resting against the barricade, when suddenly I thought I heard voices talking on the other side of the barricade – or was I dreaming? But, snatching my rifle and jumping up, I looked over the barricade and there, standing about one hundred yards away, were three Germans, quite obviously unaware that we were still holding the sunken road.

I called to them and sighted my rifle, and as I called my men immediately jumped up, grabbed their rifles and manned the barricade. The Germans instantly jumped for a ditch, along which they had crawled, but my rifle cracked and one of them lay still on its bank. Hearing the commotion at my end of the road, my officer came down the road at the run, thinking we were being attacked, but on learning the circumstances, and that two of the Germans had got away, he looked very serious and said, 'Boys, make yourselves some cover, Fritz will strafe us out of here.'

Sure enough, that afternoon Fritz was after our blood. Coming through the sky towards us we heard the unmistakable moan of a great 'coal box'.[29] Quickly we jumped into our little, hastily made dug-outs. Down from its great height, with a rush like an express train, came that terrible shell, hitting the ground a few yards from the road with a thud that almost shook down our barricade. A moment's silence and then where it had fallen the earth seemed to rise, and great lumps of earth fell all about us as we crouched down as far as possible under cover. Then, as we looked at the great crater which would nearly have held a house, we heard the distant moan of another one on its way.

Not one of us spoke; our faces were set. We knew quite well that if one of these great shells dropped at all near to us our cover would be no more use than paper and we should be blown to pieces. We just waited and hoped for the best, but Fritz was watching and getting nearer the mark. The next shell seemed to brush our little dug-outs and we could feel its hot metal as it buried itself into the far side of the road. Expecting the full blast of the explosion we held our breath and covered our faces with our arms but, thanks to God, it failed to explode: it was a dud.

Others followed, and still my little party was uninjured. Fritz slackened his firing and we were congratulating ourselves on living through such an ordeal when a shell dropped clean into the road, right on top of the men who were holding the centre part. Instantly we heard the shouts of pain and for help and we dashed madly towards the poor fellows, regardless now of all danger. The huge shell had made a fair hit. Three of the party were killed outright and the other four all wounded. Quickly we bandaged their wounds and carried them to what we thought was the safest spot. No sooner had we moved them than another shell dropped almost in the same spot as before, hurling the three dead bodies across the road.

As dusk began to fall Fritz ceased the shelling and we prepared to move the wounded men, but headquarters had witnessed the terrible time we had had, and as soon as it was dark over came stretcher bearers, expecting to find most of us either killed or wounded, and also a messenger with an order to evacuate the road and retire to our front line.

We lost no time skipping across no-man's-land and dropping into our trenches, to find there the few who were left of our battalion rebuilding up the trenches. The following night we were relieved, walking out of those bloody and battered trenches a sad, tired, badly depleted and almost officerless battalion.

The Lancashire Fusiliers had indeed lost heavily: 7 officers and 156 men had been killed, 14 officers and 298 men wounded, and 11 men were missing – heavy casualties in view of the fact that 22 officers and 675 men had been scheduled to go over the top that morning. 'The battalion fought nobly,' concludes its War Diary, 'but had no chance of success against the enemy's MG fire.' Brigadier-General Williams agreed. 'I do not think that any troops could have taken the enemy line as held on that morning,' he wrote. The German line attacked by the Lancashire Fusiliers on 1 July was eventually taken by a brigade attack, with elaborate artillery and gas support, on 13 November 1916.

Nevertheless we did not leave the trenches miles behind, to rest comfortably in some nice, quiet little village, which we naturally expected after the ordeal we had just come through. We had only reached a wood about a mile behind the trenches when the order was passed along to halt and to make ourselves as comfortable as possible in the trenches which were dug in the wood. This was a terrible disappointment and one almost wished now that he had received a wound during the advance instead of being still whole. Anyhow, cursing and wishing, we arranged our little shelters of groundsheets and pegs and settled down to a sound and much-needed sleep, the odd shells that Fritz sent into the wood not even disturbing our slumber.

We remained in the wood for a couple of days, doing practically no duties, except perhaps a trip for rations and a little rifle cleaning. Then someone in authority decided that the four battalions in our brigade could reasonably hold the front of a normal battalion, and so off we marched into the line again but this time a little to the right of our former position where, on the morning of the great advance, a Scots battalion had gone over the top and, like my own battalion, had been cut up.[30]

During the day we busied ourselves building up the battered walls of the trench and at night trying to repair the badly smashed wire defences in front of the trench. While here I received an order that I fancy was to steady my nerves again. In front of the trench in no-man's-land flowed a shallow stream and beyond that still lay dozens of dead Scots. My orders were to go out through the stream to these bodies and bring in as many rifles and identity discs as I could find. Crawling about no-man's-land in the pitch darkness, feeling around dead men's necks for discs, while Fritz swept the place with machine guns, was no joke, and needless to say not many rifles or identity discs were brought in, and the officer who gave the order for this to be done didn't trouble to come and see that it was carried out.

For about ten days we held this front and then a new battalion came to relieve us. This time our luck was in and we went right back behind the line for a complete rest, which lasted about six weeks, during which time I was acting sergeant-major for my company. New officers and drafts of men continually arrived to strengthen the battalion, and by the end of the rest we were something like a fit and fighting unit again.

After our few weeks of drilling and cleaning and peaceful nights we once more entrained for the line, eventually arriving at Poperinghe, close behind the Ypres sector. I had been on this front before and had gone to Blighty from there, wounded and gassed, and I wondered what would be my fate this time.

We settled down in camouflaged wooden huts, getting a little excitement when Fritz's planes came over to bomb us, or he sent over his long-range shells into the wood close by. We took life easy during the daytime, sleeping and writing letters, because in the night we went up into the line as working parties, riding part of the way in a train which was pulled by an engine that looked like a big, square iron box, its armoured plates covering up its usual shape. The glass windows of the carriages were all smashed and broken by shrapnel and flying fragments of shells. When Fritz got a line on the train with a battery of guns we jumped out of the carriages and into the trenches beside the track which were specially dug for this purpose.

On reaching the end of the rail journey we proceeded on foot. Our work consisted of carrying ammunition and defence materials up the line, or digging reserve, communication or cable trenches. I had only been two or three times on these working parties when fate again decreed that I should go home to England from the Ypres front.

Since my last wound at Ypres I had travelled to the fronts of Suvla Bay, Cape Helles, Egypt and the terrible Somme without a scratch. I had dodged the ravages of malaria and dysentery and the dangers of a sea infested with the terrible U-boat, and now I was to catch a bullet six hundred yards away from the enemy's line while on a working party.

We were digging a cable trench – a deep, narrow trench in which cables are laid and buried to protect them from shell fire. Each man had been allotted his task, which had to be completed before daylight. I was in charge of six men, one of whom was a lance-corporal. Work went on very well for a while, the only stoppages being for a minute or so while Fritz sprayed the place with machine-gun bullets, and once when the gas alarm sounded, which turned out to be false.

When the men had dug down a yard or so water began to settle in the bottom of the trench. It was not too cold on these nights and all the men except the lance-corporal took off their socks and carried on with their task. Of course the lance-corporal was holding up the whole party of mine so I remonstrated with him. But he insisted on being obstinate and refused to carry on and so we got to high words and even to blows. In the excitement of the scrap we both forgot the common enemy and failed to hear the warning shouts of our comrades as Fritz traversed our trench with his machine gun.

Receiving a kick like that of a horse in my left leg, I suddenly realised that bullets were flying about me and jumped quickly for the trench; almost simultaneously the lance-corporal also jumped into the trench giving a howl of pain. The next moment word was being passed along for the stretcher bearers. The lance-corporal had received a bullet in the thigh. My own left leg was going useless now and I asked the man next to me to see to it. Immediately he felt the flow of blood and the bullet hole, and again the word was passed from man to man for the stretcher bearers. Very soon these men with their stretchers were beside us. They lifted us gently out of the trench, placed bandages on our wounds, then quickly carried us away to the first-aid station, occasionally having to lie low while Fritz's infernal gun sprayed the place with lead. The first-aid station was in a cellar, all that was left of a cottage not far from where I was wounded.

As I lay there waiting my turn to be seen by the doctor the gas alarm again sounded. Quickly the orderlies placed gas masks on our faces and for half an hour we had to suffer the discomfort of the smelly gas masks along with the pain of our wounds. However, after all, it again proved to be a false alarm and quickly we were relieved of our masks, but the half-hour of breathing through the masks had finished off one poor, badly wounded comrade. Then the doctor came around to me, kneeling down beside my stretcher. He looked at the clean bullet wound through my left thigh from which the orderly had removed the temporary dressing, then half smiling he said to me, 'I will give you a fiver for it.' Quickly I answered, 'Is it a Blighty, Sir?' 'Yes,' he said. 'Then, doctor, you can't have it for five thousand,' I said. Glancing across at my recent opponent, the lance-corporal, who lay a few feet away, the doctor said, 'You are more fortunate than your regimental comrade over there. The bullet has shattered the bone of his leg.' I was very sorry to hear that and when I got the opportunity I called across to him, asking how he was feeling. He answered, 'Tray-bon, that was the best scrap I ever had,' and he smiled through his pain with that hopeful vision of going home to Blighty even at the terrible cost of a precious limb.

Before daybreak we were carried out and placed into motor ambulances and as we moved off towards Ypres stray bullets whistled over us. The driver made his way as quickly as possible out of the danger zone, along the shell-blown road, the ambulance bumping and leaping along, the axles wonderfully standing the strain, while a string of oaths and curses from the wounded passengers fell on deaf ears. But with every mile left behind the road improved and at last we stopped and were lifted out again and carried into a dressing station. Here again our wounds were redressed and the inoculation needle was stuck into our chests.

We remained here only an hour, then off again in the ambulance, halting next at Poperinghe, where our wounds were once more dressed and we were given bread and butter and tea. Then at last after the bumpy rides in the motor ambulance we were transferred into the more comfortable hospital train. Hour after hour the train steamed along. We were very comfortable and well attended to by the nurses, and as I lay watching the ever-changing view through the window I wondered if this was to be the end of my second adventure in war, and if Fritz had once again given me my ticket for home.

Darkness fell and still our carriage wheels rattled over the track joints until in the dead of night our train drew into Boulogne. Quickly we were transferred from the train into waiting motor ambulances and in a very short time we were being whizzed off along the cliffs to hospital. Here they were waiting for us. We were given a bath and dressed in a nice suit of pyjamas, tucked into bed, our wounds dressed and then we were given food and drink. Then the kind nurse told me to try and have a good night's sleep to prepare myself for the journey to England in the morning.

I was very tired and feeling clean and happy, and with my leg not giving me much pain I soon went off to sleep. It was a very troubled sleep and I needed no calling for my breakfast, after which two strapping orderlies came and lifted me gently out of bed onto a stretcher, covering me with blankets and tucking them in to make me warm and comfortable. In another few minutes I was carried from the hospital, the stretcher was secured in the ambulance and I was soon being whirled down to the docks where the hospital ship that was to take me home again was moored to the quay. Down the gangway of the ship I was carefully carried and taken to a deck below that looked exactly like a hospital ward.

Nurses were busy attending to the wants of the sick and wounded and we hardly noticed the ship start on her way, hardly thought of the sea or submarines. The journey across the channel was quite uneventful and during the passage each man was asked which county he would like to go to on arriving in England. The government by this time was trying to get every wounded man into hospital as near to his own home as possible. Of course I said I wished to go to my native Lancashire, and a huge number four was written on my medical card.

About five o'clock that evening we sailed into Southampton and as quickly as possible we were transferred to our respective ambulance trains waiting at the quayside. Soon the engine of my train was puffing away, eating up the miles northwards, its destination being Manchester, eighteen miles from my home town. As usual, we were very comfortable in the train, the nurses continually asking if we were all right or required anything, and we lay looking through the broad carriage windows at the scenery that was beginning to fade now in the gathering dusk, and thinking how good it was to be back once again in the British Isles.

From dusk it went to dark and still the wheels below us spun round until with a grinding of brakes we were awakened from a half-sleep to find the train coming to a stop in a large station – Birmingham. During our short stay in the platform a parson hurriedly made his way from one man to another, carrying a bundle of printed postcards on which he quickly wrote each man's address and destination, and also whether wounded or sick. Then as the train moved off again he hurried to post the whole lot. Incidentally, the postcard this parson sent for me was the first notice to my parents that I was wounded and so near to them.

By midnight we had reached Manchester and after a quick transference into waiting ambulances in a few minutes we were being carried to beds in a school at Lower Broughton which had been turned into a temporary hospital. I soon let them know at home of my whereabouts, and as quickly they were on the train and soon sitting by my bedside, forcing on me dainties and luxuries I had not had for months and months.

My second journey home to Blighty must have been almost a record and one could hardly believe it possible that within forty-eight hours I was brought wounded from the trenches at Ypres to this school at Lower Broughton. With careful dressing and good attention my leg quickly healed up and very soon I was up, and when the weather was nice I went out for a walk in the park close by with the aid of a couple of sticks, and later I was able to push along a wounded comrade in an invalid chair.

Beds were urgently wanted and I was marked fit to leave hospital. I asked to go to a convalescent camp for a while before having the usual leave, but only having been to the front twice and thousands not yet having been at all the doctor must have thought that I was better suited to go again and therefore marked me A1. I was given a railway ticket to my home and ten days' leave after which I was to report again to my regiment's training camp at Withernsea. My second leave at home since the commencement of the war passed over all too quickly. I had a great time and my leg did wonderfully, and then having got away from the tears and heartbreaking farewells of relatives and friends I again found myself back in the ranks drilling, route-marching, and training for the horrible business over in France.

I did not feel too happy, and my heart was bitter against war and everyone connected with it, and after two doses I was rather jealous of the man in the cushy jobs. I could see my third trip to Flanders materialising in the very near future and I felt quite sure that 'the third time would pay for all'.

Some of the officers and NCOs in camp and in charge had seen service in France, and returned either sick or wounded, and they made quite sure that at least neglect of duty would not send them back to Flanders, therefore woe betide the defaulter. Malingering was against my nature and deserting would be, and would bring too big a disgrace on my parents. Anyhow, my sourness soon got my name on the list for a draft to France. I had suffered two wounds, had a bad dose of poison gas, a couple of frozen feet, and endured the agonies of dysentery, but in ten seconds I was marked fit for active service by the MO.

6

Return to France

The usual preparations, the train journey, the trip on the cattle-boat – another trip like many I had had before in the rattling cattle-trucks – a march, and we arrived at the famous and dreaded base camp at Étaples. What a name to remember for any infantryman unfortunate enough to have to stay there a few days: its bullying and cowardly officers and NCOs in charge, its arrogant military police, and its 'Bull Ring' – a name that inspired more hatred and dread in a Tommy than did the name of Ypres itself.[31]

The Bull Ring – a great circle of trenches and barbed wire and sacks of sawdust, where men in full fighting kit ran and charged and stabbed with fixed bayonets until almost exhausted, tormented at the same time with personal insults from the well fed, polished up and swaggering sergeant in charge, until one rather weakling Aussie, unable to stand the strain and torture, and sensitive to the insults hurled at him, saved just enough strength for one big thrust with his bayonet, a thrust deep into the stomach of the bullying NCO.

As he lay groaning and dying on the floor we men – who had held on to the four-mile stretch of Gallipoli or the churned up ridge of Passchendaele – were formed up and marched back to camp, where we were confined, and men with machine guns and rifles surrounded our tents like warders round a party of prisoners who had tried to escape. Even the little town of Étaples beside our camp was put out of bounds to us. Its cafés and mademoiselles were only for the well groomed, well fed staff in their safe and cushy jobs.

But jail-like regulations and red tape only fanned a flame of hatred against the commandant and the military police and the resultant kick over the traces soon came – an organised breakaway, the police roughly handled, those of them who were mounted galloping away for their lives. An ugly situation. Men in an ugly mood, tempers risen high, recklessly swarming out of camp, caring nought for the consequences. Fighting men were not going to be treated like convicts.

The authorities treated the matter in the safest way. They posted up huge lists of names of men to be prepared for the line. The trenches were the best place for these wild men of Flanders.

We bid farewell to Étaples and its famous Bull Ring, and after long, horrible hours of riding and marching we stood in front of the Adjutant of the 16th Lancashire Fusiliers, a Salford Pals Battalion in the 32nd Division. We were fortunate in joining this battalion just as they had come out of the line for a long rest. I was detailed to A Company, and being a corporal I was put in charge of a section of men. My boys at first were inclined to treat me with contempt, but when they found that I was no dud on active service they soon obeyed and respected me.

The 16th (Service) Battalion the Lancashire Fusiliers, known as the 2nd Salford Battalion, was raised on 5 November 1914, with three companies from Salford and one from Eccles. It crossed to France in November 1915, and like so many other New Army battalions was engaged on the first day of the Somme, when it lost 8 officers and 223 men in an abortive attack on Thiepval, just across the Ancre from Beaumont Hamel where the 1st Battalion was so sorely tried. The attack was pressed with fruitless determination because of an erroneous report that elements of 15th Lancashire Fusiliers – the 1st Salfords – had got into Thiepval and needed help. The battalion was repeatedly in action on the Somme, and Ashurst joined it shortly before it moved south in February 1917 as part of a general extension of the British line into a sector previously held by the French. In march, however, it was on the move again, following up the German withdrawal to the Hindenburg line. The commanding officer was Lieutenant-Colonel C. M. Abercrombie CMG, who had commanded the battalion from its formation, having previously been adjutant of the 15th Battalion.

I had been with the battalion only a few days and the colonel hardly knew I was there, but he found out only too well during the next few days. We were billeted in leaky-roofed old barns and tents and the battalion was anything but comfortable. At this time the army had just started to use the Nissen hut, a rainbow-shaped hut, big enough to house 30 or 40 men comfortably. Our colonel was determined to have his men properly rested and sheltered and he applied for sufficient huts to shelter the battalion. One NCO and four men were detailed off to go to the next village and learn from the Engineers how to build these sectional huts. I was the NCO selected, and the four men, one from each of the four companies, were the four biggest duds in the battalion – the four company sergeant-majors, as was usual, selecting the biggest dud as a soldier for a working party.

I marched my four men off and we made our way to the next village, where I reported to the officer in charge of the Engineers. At once I was helping and learning how to build Nissen huts but my men had been sent to a nearby wood and were busy cutting down trees, from the trunks of which were cut the foundations for the huts. The huts consisted of six wooden floor sections placed in position on legs driven into the ground. Then rainbow-shaped iron frames were bolted to the floors. Each end of the hut was built up in one piece, one end being composed of the door and windows. The roof of the hut was sheets of corrugated iron bolted to the frames and then linked with tongued and grooved timber.

A couple of days with the Engineers and I knew all there was to be known about the building of Nissen huts. On the other hand, my men, who had made excellent lumbermen, knew absolutely nothing about the building of huts. Back again with the battalion the sections of these huts we were to build were being quickly delivered to us and the building commenced. There was one builder – myself – and four labourers on the job.

We had no saws, no hammers, no nails or spanners, and the very trees we needed for the foundations we were forbidden to cut down. The colonel, I am sure, had no idea what kind of huts they were or what was needed to build them. Anyhow, we managed to get hold of a saw and with our entrenching tools and a lot of dodging when the old French farmer was about we managed to secure the foundations for our first hut, and drove them into the ground. The first hut built was to house the quartermaster and his stores and rations.

On the second day of our labours around came the colonel. I was standing on a ration box inside our first Nissen hut fixing in the tongued and grooved timbers. The colonel walked straight towards me and tailing on behind him was the adjutant, the regimental sergeant-major, the quartermaster, the orderly sergeant and several other nonentities. Glaring at me, the colonel rapped out rather sharply and angrily, 'Corporal, what is the meaning of this, your men hanging around doing nothing and you haven't yet completed one hut, and been at the job two days. I am given to understand that one of these huts should be put up in two hours. It is evident to me you cannot control your men.'

On hearing these words my blood boiled. I had been in charge of men in the front line long before the formation of this colonel's battalion, and staring defiantly at the colonel I said, 'Sir, allow me to inform you that I was controlling men before your battalion was formed.' The colonel speechless, the adjutant turned pale, and a deathly silence prevailed for a few moments as I and the colonel stood glaring at each other. I think during those few moments I was as near being shot as ever I had been in the front line trenches, but quickly recovering from the shock the colonel rapped out. 'Place this man under arrest', and turning on his heel he walked out of the half-finished hut and I found myself in the charge of a sergeant who was my close companion until the following morning, when I appeared at the battalion orderly room to answer for my breach of discipline.

A few of the boys went in first on minor charges. Then the sergeant-major's voice bawled out, 'Corporal Ashurst – cap off – left turn – quick march – right turn – Halt.' I was again face to face with the colonel. The adjutant began to read out the charge but the colonel cut him short and, looking at me, he asked, 'Where did you get your first stripe?' I answered, 'With the 3rd Battalion Lancashire Fusiliers at camp in Wales in July 1914, Sir.' 'And who promoted you to full corporal?' he asked again. I replied, 'Colonel Magniac of the 1st Lancashire Fusiliers, Sir.' 'Oh, I know Colonel Magniac, a fine soldier,' he said.

Then the colonel asked me why it was taking so long to put up the Nissen huts. He said that he was most anxious to get the battalion under decent cover before their return to the trenches. I then informed him that my four men were the biggest duds in the battalion. The colonel immediately sent for the four company sergeant-majors to verify my statement. This the sergeant-majors did, explaining that it was the usual procedure to pick out the worst soldiers for working parties.

Then I explained to the colonel how the engineer officer had sent my men off to cut down trees, saying that one NCO was sufficient to see how the huts were built. I also explained how necessary it was for me to have saws and spanners, etc., and that the very trees I required for foundations for the huts I was forbidden to cut down.

When I had finished my story I could see that the colonel was enlightened and impressed and he said, 'All right, Corporal, I will forgive you your insubordination. Now let's get down to this hut business. I am determined that these huts shall be put up quickly at all costs.' Then the colonel told me that the battalion pioneers would be at my service with their tools, and he asked me how many men I could reasonably employ on the job. I told him that I could easily keep a score of men busy on the huts, and he turned to the adjutant and told him to make it possible to procure the trees I required. Then I was dismissed the charge against me and the work on the Nissen huts began in earnest.

In a few day's time, with all these resources at my command, the whole battalion was almost under cover. Once again the colonel came around, but this time to congratulate me on the speed the huts were going up, and a couple of weeks later I was promoted by my colonel to the rank of sergeant.

The rest was soon over and the serious business came round again. Up into the line and once more the old routine of sentry-go, bombing raids, sniping and working parties. Aeroplanes were more active now and it was an everyday occurrence to see the large, cream-coloured English planes with the big red, white and blue targets painted on the wings engaging the whiter-looking planes of the Germans with a huge black iron cross as their distinguishing mark. Our observation plane flew along the front for hours at a stretch, its observer keenly watching the enemy and the effect of our artillery fire, also at the same time keeping his machine gun ready to blaze away at any approaching enemy plane.

Behind us, in the distance, floating high in the sky were huge sausage-like observation balloons, anchored down to motor lorries on which were winches with which the balloons could be wound in and run along to another front at short notice. Fritz often caused a lot of excitement by his frequent lightning raids at these balloons. Suddenly, dropping from behind a cloud where he had been hiding, he would swoop at the balloon, blazing away with his machine gun and sending a stream of incendiary bullets into the huge envelope. The observation officer in the basket quickly jumped out, released his parachute and floated down to earth, the big balloon following him a few moments afterwards in a mass of flames.

The German airman, having done his work of destruction, flew madly back for the German lines, followed by a trail of powder smoke from the shells of our anti-aircraft guns. One evening just as darkness was coming on a German plane made a sudden raid on three of these huge balloons. Very soon one of them was coming down in flames. Still Fritz flew straight for the next one, anti-aircraft guns thundering away at him. Machine guns and rifles pumped bullets into the sky about him, but as though charmed the plane circled about each one in turn and completely destroyed all three of them, then returned safely and triumphantly over the German lines, almost in darkness. Just another German airman whose chest would surely be adorned with an Iron Cross.

We were continually changing our front these days. I think it was partly to puzzle Fritz regarding our movements and numbers. Still, whatever the cause, it entailed a lot of hard marching for us. Men fell exhausted as we marched along, and were sometimes brutally pushed a little farther by the comfortably mounted adjutant threatening to gallop his horse on their prostrate bodies. As I marched by the men, listening to the horrible wishes and curses, I wondered what fear it was that kept them, armed as they were, from turning on such tyranny and quickly taking vengeance. There was no doubt that every battalion had its malingerers, but the thought of malingering was too much in the mind of some officers. When the real test of duty and courage came I can vouch that the percentage of malingerers amongst the men was comparable to that of the officers.

At the end of thse marches there was not a comfortable meal and bed. We were fortunate to get inside an old French barn where we could drop our heavy packs and rifles on to the straw causing, the rats to scurry off and find fresh lodgings temporarily, and take our heavy, muddy boots off sore and bleeding feet. One or two of the fittest men would volunteer to go to the quartermaster for whatever rations there were, while another two would be off to the field kitchens for a dixie of greasy tea. Then as we sat on the straw eating a lump of bread and a piece of fried bacon that had been skimmed at you with a pair of dirty hands, some wise guy would inform us that through the careless or faulty reading of some officer we had marched about four miles farther than we need have done.

During one of these breaks from the trenches I was sent down the line on an NCOs' special training course. Off I went, miles behind the line, to a little village where this school was situated. On arrival I found most cosy billets – a wooden hut with a big stove and wooden beds and straw mattresses and pillows for each man, where we could undress and lie down nice and warm under great army blankets and sleep soundly, undisturbed by the crunch of 5.9s. Pay was regular, and a good feed or a drink could be had at several places in the village. We paraded daily, clean and refreshed, to learn map reading, musketry, bombing and also billeting, marching off to nearby villages and estimating and calculating the number of troops that could be billeted in the cottages and barns and public buildings. How happy I was one can imagine, this being my third time in France after having had experiences also in Eygpt and the Dardenelles.

I had grown heartily tired of trenches and war so one can guess my sorrow when the course was finished and I was on my way back to the front once again. However, back again with the boys I soon forgot what comfort was and settled down in the old grousing mood.

I had not been back with the battalion many days when we were ordered to move right down south and take over on a front held by the French. Certain of our officers and NCOs went on ahead of the battalion to see and get to know all about this new front. They had to dress as French soldiers while doing this so that Fritz would not know of the change until we got opposite him. When we eventually took over the front we found there were excellent dug-outs; it was such a quiet spot and to all appearances the French had been having quite a soft time of it. In fact some of our boys said that there were actually beaten tracks from our front line to that of the Germans. Anyhow, Fritz was not long in finding out that English troops were opposite to him, and when he did the fun started and 'heads down' was once again the motto.

When going out resting from this front we marched back a few miles behind the line and then suddenly disappeared down a hole in the middle of a field, walking down fifty or sixty steps past a wet-blanketed gas-proof door into an enormous dug-out that ran underground for hundreds of yards and was timbered at the top, sides and bottom. It contained wire-netting beds made in two decks, on which were straw mattresses and pillows, where we could sleep undisturbed by the great shells Fritz sent over.

One night while we were in the line word came down from Battalion Headquarters that a raid on the German front line had to be made. Our company had to supply the raiding party and I was one of the NCOs selected for it. Down into the dug-out we went to black our faces and get bombs ready. We were waiting for the order to go when another messenger dashed down into the dug-out, calling out that the raid was off and that Fritz had left his trenches and flown. We thought the man was mad, but he assured us that what he said was correct.

115

We dashed up into the trenches and, true enough, men were jumping on top of the trenches and others were out in no-man's-land. Odd bullets whistled over from Fritz's lines, but nothing to trouble about. Right ahead, well behind the German lines, great red glares lit up the sky. It appeared that during the night our patrols had been right over to the German trenches and found them deserted except for a few odd snipers who had been left behind to make believe that Fritz still occupied them. These snipers soon gave themselves up as prisoners at the approach of our men.

For several months the Germans had been preparing a new line some twenty-five miles behind the Somme front, and in March 1917 they withdrew to the new position – called the Hindenburg Line by the Allies – relinquishing the huge salient which had bulged out between Arras and Soissons. The retirement has rightly been termed a master stroke, for it exchanged a bad, haphazard line for a well prepared and carefully sited one. It also wrong-footed the forthcoming Allied offensive, the brain-child of the new French commander-in-chief, General Robert Nivelle. The resultant failure of the Nivelle offensive was the last straw for the French army, part of which mutinied. But to George Ashurst and the 16th Lancashire Fusiliers the immediate problem was following up the German withdrawal across a blighted landscape.

All was activity now in our trenches. Kits were packed up and everything was got ready for a quick move forward. Of course rumours were soon flying about that the war was over and Fritz was off back to Germany. If it could only be true! But the people who did have an idea what was happening kept their knowledge to themselves. All that Tommy was allowed to know was what he could see for himself on his own front. Anyhow, it was a little cheering to know that the Germans were retiring and not advancing.

By the break of day we were ready to go after Fritz. Scouts had gone on ahead and were keeping in touch with the enemy's rearguard. Out in no-man's-land we actually fell in by platoons and moved off – on over Fritz's deserted front line and reserve trenches, marching steadily on while at intervals long-range shells would come humming over our heads, just chance shots from Fritz hoping for a lucky hit. On we went, ready at a moment's notice to open out for action at a sign from the scouts in front.

The further we went the more we saw of what a ruthless retreating army can do. Telegraph poles were cut down and laid across the roads and into the cut and straggling wires had been woven branches of trees and thorny bushes. Huge trees, and in some places whole avenues of them, had been hacked down and brought crashing across the roads, making them impossible to use, and we had to take to the fields on either side.

The centre of crossroads had been mined and blown up, leaving great, gaping craters twenty or thirty feet deep. Canal and river bridges had been blown to bits and railway lines blown up beyond repair, Fritz having placed a detonation every yard or so along the track. Wells had been poisoned and we were warned not to drink any water except that issued from our own water carts. Fritz had set traps for us in all sorts of odd places and we were continually on the look out for strings and wires that might easily have been attached to hidden bombs. Tempting articles and objects were laid about to catch the unwary, and men were afraid to enter shelters or dug-outs in case they were death traps.

When we arrived at a village there was nothing left except the black ruins – no shelter at all but the damp dirty cellars that might have escaped the flames. Later we found that Fritz was burning five villages out of six and then cramming the old people and the children out of the five he had burned into the sixth, making two-decker wire-netting beds in the cottages on which the extra people could sleep, and as he decamped he left the poor souls with a little watery soup for food – telling them that the English would be coming and that we should give them more – which prophecy was quite true, but the boys had to go on half rations to give the other half to the villagers.

As we approached one of these villages the villagers came out to meet us, cheering, kissing us and shaking our hands, lots of them with tears running down their cheeks. These people had lived under the Germans for nearly three years and soon we were listening to horrible stories of bayonetted fathers and sons and outraged mothers and daughters; of cruelties almost unbelievable of a civilised nation.[32]

In the village there was a notable shortage of young men and women. On asking why, we were told that they had gone with Fritz. Not a horse or cow or sheep or fowl of any description was left in the village, and dogs and cats were conspicuous by their absence. The little cottage gardens had been stripped bare of every vegetable, and even the little berry trees had been cut down level with the ground. One such village I remember was called Nesle and the boys said that this must be where the tinned milk came from.

Engineers were close on our heels and soon had temporary bridges built across rivers and canals, while the field guns and ammunition and ration wagons lumbered on marvellously quickly behind us. We were on top of Fritz's rearguard now and pressing him hard, and at the next railway cutting he had decided to stop and fight a rearguard action, to check us for a while. He had turned a few batteries of field guns on to us and kept up a brisk fire. We spread out and advanced a few yards at a time in quick, short rushes. When we were easily within range Fritz opened out with machine-gun and rifle fire, spreading a hail of bullets across the fields, but down we went into any hole or ditch there was about. There was not a lot of cover, however, and we were getting it pretty hot, losing quite a number of men.

117

Nevertheless, Fritz had to be moved, and forward we went, getting nearer and nearer to the cutting until the Germans, realising that we were not to be stopped, suddenly took to their heels, leaving us the cutting and also a little dog which had been shot through the haunches. Of course the little fellow was soon bandaged up and in a short time was running about the cutting showing no desire to return to Fritz – probably he preferred good English bully beef to German black bread and sausages.

After this engagement it was decided to rest our battalion, and fresher troops coming up from behind pushed on after Fritz. Our battalion then settled for a while in a burnt-out village, the men picking out the best of the cellars to live in.[33] My company was fortunate in getting quartered in an almost undamaged château, standing in its own great, lovely grounds, which the Germans had been using up to their evacuation as a field hospital. My own platoon was billeted in what had been the kitchen of the great house but I and the other three sergeants of the company selected a nice little cellar complete with stove which we found in the building.

During the first day of our rest we were employed filling in the huge craters at the village crossroads, piling in tree trunks and bricks from the burnt cottages, or dragging anything at all to the hole that would help to fill it up quickly so that our transports and guns could get on after the Germans.

That same afternoon one or two of our men were found lying about the village absolutely drunk, then others were discovered in the same intoxicated state in their billets. Immediately our officers were looking around and enquiring the cause and they found that some of the men had discovered a well filled wine cellar that had escaped the eyes of the Germans from the start of the war. A guard was soon placed on the cellar and the wine, too rich for Tommy, was transferred to the officers' quarters. However, this find of wine had suggested to the boys the idea of buried treasure and there started a regular treasure hunt in the village, and not without good result.

More and more treasure was found – household treasures that had been buried and hidden on the first, swift advance of the Germans at the start of the war. The boys hacked down walls and dug up floors and passages, working with pick and shovel on anything that seemed to show any kind of unusual mark or sign. Bundles of notes, cash, jewellery, ornaments, musical instruments, cutlery, bundles of bedding and clothes and every conceivable thing of value were found. Buried treasure was the whole topic of conversation; the search for it was not considered as looting, or the treasure as loot, for which every man on active service knew that the penalty was death.[34]

That evening as I and the other three sergeants had dismissed our batmen and settled down for the night on the floor of our little cellar, with the stove burning brightly. We also talked of buried treasure, and Sergeant Faller suddenly said, 'Listen.' We other three listened, and Faller's voice broke out again. 'There is sure to be some treasure, and where I'll bet nobody has looked yet. I have got a little scheme. We four could work nicely tonight.' And as we lay there on our groundsheets covered with a blanket and overcoat, our feet tucked into our tunic sleeves, we listened to Faller's idea.

He began, 'You know the long drive leading from the village road to this house? Did you notice the family burial vault about half-way down the drive and standing about twenty yards to one side, amongst the rhododendron bushes?' We listeners caught our breath. 'Well,' continued Faller, 'the man who owned this place must have been rich, and these French people bury their dead adorned in their rings and jewellery.'

The drift of Faller's scheme began to dawn on us now and he was brought to a halt by exclamations of doubt and disagreement. But Faller, disgust at our fear in his voice, bawled out, 'Are you afraid of dead men? Why, I have shaved them and they have groaned at me when I've leaned on their chest to shave their chins better.' I said, 'What if we are caught at this game. Do you know the penalty, and do you know that a sentry from my platoon is patrolling the drive?'

'Yes,' said Faller. 'That's where your job comes in, so listen and don't interrupt again. Your job is to keep that sentry of yours engaged and far enough away from the vault while I and the other two get inside it, and then make your way to the vault as best you can.' And Faller, jumping up, began to get ready for the job, unwillingly followed by the other three of us. So, lighting the stump of a candle, the four of us prepared for our treasure hunt.

'Stick a candle in one of your pockets and I will bring along this entrenching tool,' said Faller. When all was ready I moved off alone, making straight to the drive to do my part. As I walked along I could hear the sentry whistling softly on his beat and then, as I approached nearer to him, he heard my footsteps and pointing his rifle straight at me he shouted, 'Halt, who goes there?' 'It's all right, Green,' I said. 'It's the sergeant.'

Recognising my voice, Green said, 'Hello, Sergeant, what's to do? Can't you sleep?' 'Oh, yes,' I said, 'but I wanted to warn you that the orderly officer is on the prowl tonight, and I don't want him to catch my sentry napping.' 'Thanks, Sergeant,' said Green. 'I'll see he don't do it on me.' 'Good,' I said, 'come on, Green, I'll have a walk as far as the road with you.' I handed Green a cigarette and told him to have a smoke, but to give the cigarette quickly back to me should we hear anyone approaching.

Slowly we walked to the road and I kept up a conversation to try and drown from the ears of Green any noise that Faller and the others might make in their scramble through the bushes. On reaching the road at the end of the drive I kept Green busy talking and enjoying his smoke a little longer until I felt sure that Faller and the others were safely inside the vault. Then, bidding Green goodnight, I walked off quickly down the drive as if going straight back to my little cellar, but half-way down the drive I stopped and listened. Green had not yet started his return to the château, and quickly I dived through the bushes, making my way as quickly and silently as possible to the family vault.

Arriving at the iron-studded door of the vault I found it open about an inch. I called softly, 'Hello, Faller.' Instantly a whispered command came back from inside the vault: 'Come on in and close the door behind you.' I pushed the heavy door open slowly and walked into pitch-black darkness, shoving the heavy door to again as I stood there seeing absolutely nothing. Then Faller whispered, and, drawing us together in the darkness by feeling for us, he told us to search the floor for a trapdoor. I must confess that I did not do much searching myself and I do not know what searching the other two did, but it was quite evident that Faller had wasted no time for a muttered exclamation from him told us that he had been successful.

Again he clutched at our clothes in the darkness and whispered, 'Follow me, and the last man close the door behind him.' Faller felt his way down the cold stone steps and obediently we followed, keeping in touch with each other. My heart was thumping hard now as my hands felt the cold stone and my nostrils filled with a damp, earthy smell. I should not have been surprised if suddenly, out of the black stillness, a chevalier of bygone days, with huge sword in hand, had appeared to bar our progress, but the heavy breathing of some other mortal under great strain and the angry whispered voice of Faller calling, 'Shut that —— door' kept me to earth. Then again Faller's voice, in an angry whisper, asked 'Is that —— door shut?' 'Yes,' I managed to call softly back to him without biting my tongue.

'Where is that candle? Make a light quick, you duds,' came again the quiet command of Faller through the inky blackness. There was nervously whispered dissention, but Faller's voice came quietly but firmly again: 'Make a light, no one can see us now.' A match scraped on the stone step, and the candle-light spluttered in. Our eyes were dazzled by it for a while and then its flickering circle of light showed the four of us, faces grim and pale, standing at the foot of a flight of stone steps in a kind of bare stone hall. On our right was what must have been the burial chamber. A passage was left open down the middle of it and on either side hung great white curtains on which was woven in black silk French inscriptions which we did not understand.

We stared at them in awe and then Faller walked to one of the curtains and looked behind it. I fully expected something to happen to him and I hardly dared to watch him when an exclamation from Faller drew my attention, and there he stood holding in his arms what looked like a black violin case, and motioning to us to come nearer with the candle.

As we automatically moved up to him he placed the case on the floor and was soon forcing open the lid with the entrenching tool he had brought with him. Soon the lid was smashed open and a gasp of admiration broke from us as the contents of the case were revealed. There in the plush-lined case rested a beautiful gold cross inlaid with precious stones that glittered in the flickering candle-light. Faller gave an exclamation of delight. 'Sparklers, boys,' he said, 'real sparklers.' Quickly closing up the lid of the case he said, 'Come on back to the cellar, quick.'

This order was carried out silently but with alacrity: the trap door was closed again, the carpet replaced, and then we waited impatiently until the sentry on his lonely beat had passed the vault and was well on towards the end of the drive again. Then quickly we slid by the iron door again and, bent double, we threaded our way quietly through the trees and bushes back to our cosy little cellar.

The fire in the little stove still burned and in its light we began to examine our treasure. There were doubts about the genuineness of the stones but Faller, flirting them out of their resting place in the cross with his jack-knife, placed some of them between his fingers and, waving his hand in the firelight said, 'Look, boys, don't you know real sparklers when you see them? There are hundreds of quids' worth here, hundreds I tell you, – and his eyes sparkled like the stones. When the huge diamonds and rubies and emeralds had been torn out of the gold, the share-out began.

The first to receive a share of the spoils was the little stove. Carefully it was given every little bit of the black case until not the smallest piece was left. Then, after a thorough stocktaking, Faller made four equal little heaps of red, white and green stones. 'What about the cross?' asked someone, 'what shall we do with that – throw it in the river?' 'Indeed not,' said Faller. 'We can't afford to throw away yellow gold like that.' He took up his entrenching tool and began to break up the cross into small pieces, muttering as he did it that 'good gold was fairly soft'. Soon four little heaps of gold pieces were carefully picked up and tucked away with the precious stones.

A solemn pledge of secrecy was made and we settled down to sleep for the rest of the night. I certainly had a troubled night's sleep, and judging from the uneasy movements of the others they too were anything but sound asleep, with the exception of Faller, from whose corner came a steady, deep snore, a snore of untroubled nerves and restful sleep.

We were disturbed from a late slumber by a shout of 'Breakfast up, Sergeants' from our batman, who had arrived from the cookhouse with the bacon and tea. We just sat up and lazily held out our mess tins while the batman poured in some tea then, dipping a piece of bread in the fat and grabbing a piece of bacon with our unwashed hands, we dined and talked, being careful not to mention the night's adventure in the presence of the batman.

After breakfast we tidied up a little and made out way to our different platoons. My platoon officer came along to see the men just as I arrived at their billet and as we stood watching the men clean up their billet a motor car came slowly down the drive. A French military chauffeur sat at the wheel. The car came to a stand in the courtyard of the château and out jumped an English staff officer, followed by a French staff officer and a French civilian. Instantly I sensed that the civilian was the owner of the place, and my mind went back to the escapade of the night, causing me to feel a little uneasy.

My officer walked up to them and saluted. I also edged a little nearer and tried to catch their conversation but they spoke quickly in French and I was no wiser as to their mission. The civilian looked around at the buildings and smiled, making some remark to his companions. Then he walked into the place where my platoon had spent the night.

The visitors had only been inside a few moments when my officer called me and told me to clear the whole platoon and their kit outside, with the exception of two men. These two men were despatched to the quartermaster's stores for a pick and shovel, and on returning with these implements, to the consternation of myself and my platoon, they were set to work digging up the kitchen floor. On removing a couple of flags and a layer of earth these two men began to uncover brown-paper and wash-leather parcels. These were quickly transferred to the waiting motor car under the staring eyes of my men. One can imagine the look on their faces, and the expressions they uttered, as they realised that they had been sleeping on the greatest hidden treasure of all.

The parcels having been safely transferred to the waiting car, the civilian came out of the building and my heart again beat fast as he walked straight to the family vault, pushing open the heavy iron door and going inside, where he saw that a great beautiful, gilded angel and the huge marble slab it stood upon had been smashed to pieces by some spiteful German. However, after a few moments' inspection he came out with a smile on his face. He got into the car, followed by the staff officers, and they all drove away – much to my relief.

After a couple of days at the château we were off again in pursuit of the enemy. Other troops were close on the Germans' heels and we were fast catching up to them, which we eventually did on the outskirts of St Quentin. Here Fritz had determined to make a stand. We took up our position on a rise on the left of the town. In front of St Quentin were the French and some of their foreign troops, whom we could watch quite plainly going over the top and trying to take the old town without the use of artillery.

I don't know if it was quite true but the rumour was about that the French wished to take the town without shelling it but Fritz was firmly fixed in the houses with his machine guns, and played havoc with them amongst the attackers. However, our own front concerned us most and that evening we were told off in support of a battalion of famous Scottish soldiers who were going over the top on a silent raid.

The night was black and just the kind for a raid of that description. The Jocks had been gone some time and quickly and silently we went over after them to hold the position they had taken. We reached the German lines quite easily and found that the Scottish laddies had done their terrible work only too well. Dozens of Germans were lying about the trenches bayoneted to death. They had been caught napping all right, having been done to death as they lay in their shallow dug-outs; some of them had died as they made desperate efforts to leave the trenches.

When daylight came a ghastly sight met our eyes. I felt quite sorry for these poor fellows and thought of Fritz's retribution when those who had got away informed him of the fate of their comrades. We would get it quick and hot, I had not the slightest doubt. Anyhow, we collected the dead bodies of the Germans together and laid them side by side in a sunken road that ran near the trench. There we dug one huge, shallow grave and laid them in it side by side. One body in particular took my eye. It was that of a youth of no more than sixteen years, a good-looking lad in spite of death in his face, with lovely blond hair. He had just had time to place his hand over his stomach before a Scottish bayonet had gone deep to its terrible work. He had a photo in his pocket – a group of four people whom I judged to be his father and mother, his sister or sweetheart, and himself. I placed the photo against his heart and as I gently placed him in his grave beside his comrades I knew that a terrible blow was shortly coming to someone waiting hopefully back in Germany.

That day Fritz set his guns to the range of our trenches. We knew we should get it and it had come. Whiz-bang after whiz-bang, travelling with lightning speed, fell about our shallow trench and the sunken road; great, black high-explosive shrapnel shells that seemed to rend the sky asunder burst over our heads, spraying the whole place with hot metal. Huge howitzer shells came moaning out of the sky, making great craters, scattering earth and stones for hundreds of yards and shaking the trenches like an earthquake.

We crouched in the small shelters dug into the sides of the trench, but one expected every moment to be blown to pieces or at least to feel the blow and burning pain of a piece of hot metal. Men were calling out for help, lying in agony, but to move about in those trenches or that sunken road was asking for certain death.

After a while our own guns in the rear began to roar, and speedily pumped shells over to Fritz's lines, giving him a hot time of it, which brought a welcome respite for us. But Fritz had had his revenge; our casualties were heavy and our position considerably weakened. Anyhow, the wounded were quickly attended to and with fast and hard work transferred to the rear, while the dead were quickly and silently buried.

As that day wore on rumour ran around that we were to advance and go over the top the following morning at dawn. Spirits were low; death was about everywhere; our position was a precarious one. We knew that we were in for a very hot time of it and one almost felt that death would at least be a relief from it all.

However, fate played one of its strange tricks, at least with myself and a few of the boys. During the afternoon a messenger made his way gingerly but quickly along the old road; his message was for me. I had to report to the adjutant at once. I asked the messenger what I was wanted at headquarters for but he knew nothing and, with my heart pumping fast and wondering what ever was in store for me, I made my way along the narrow trenches to the headquarters dug-out.

The adjutant told me that it was our battalion's turn to supply the divisional general's guard, and that through my length of service in the line and my merits as an NCO I had been chosen as sergeant of this guard. He told me that one corporal and nine men would be selected and detailed under my charge, and that it was a great honour to me and that he hoped I would uphold the good name of my regiment before the general.[35]

Thanking him for the honour and promising that I would not let the regiment down, I saluted and made my way back to the company, skipping down the communication trenches as light as a ballet dancer, hardly daring to think of my wonderful luck. Back at my post I told the boys of my good fortune and while they congratulated me they fervently hoped that they would be one of my guard. Quickly I packed my kit and was ready to move again to headquarters to collect my men. I bade the boys farewell and good luck and searched out the sergeants of my sparkler escapade. Shaking hands with them I wished them the best of luck and hoped to be with them again when the general's guard was over, but Faller said quite solemnly, 'I think this is my last trip over the top.' 'Stop it – none of that,' we all yelled simultaneously, but Faller insisted: 'Yes, its my last trip – I feel sure of it.' 'Bah,' I said, 'I'll be seeing you after the guard', and smiling at him as I moved away I felt rather queer myself to see the carefree Faller looking strangely despondent.[36]

Arriving once again at headquarters I collected my guard and as we quickly made our way to the battalion quartermaster's stores, the first stopping place from that hell hole, our hearts and packs seemed strangely light. Talking and joking happily, we jogged along, now a few miles from that dreaded line, taking no notice at all of the odd shells that seemed to be making a last effort to get us before we were out of reach. Eventually we reached the stores and were issued with clean under-clothes, suits and equipment. We had a jolly good wash and feed before we donned them. The general's headquarters were still a good number of miles away but we were not due there until the following day so we settled down for the night at the stores, and for once in a while we had more bedding and blankets than we really needed.

Next morning, feeling fine after a good night's rest, we washed, shaved and had a good brush-up, and looked like real peacetime soldiers as we sat down to an extra good breakfast prepared by the storekeeper. When all were ready we set off for the château where the general had his headquarters. As we marched along we talked of the attack our boys had made that morning. We all knew very well that the boys were in for a hot time, and Sergeant Faller's words – it's my last trip – seemed to ring in my ears. I wondered if it had been.

At the château I reported to the general's aide-de-camp and he soon explained our duties to me. A couple of tents in the grounds of the château close by the entrance from the road were to be our home for the next six weeks. One of my men was detailed as servant to the remainder of the guard, doing all the dirty work and tidying up the tents, looking to meals, etc. This man was always conspicuous by his absence at the turn-out of the guards and did no sentry duty. One man only was on sentry duty, on the gates at the entrance to the château for a stretch of two hours. Therefore the guard was very easy, the men having two hours on sentry duty and fourteen hours off. The whole guard turned out once per day, spick and span. This was for the general himself when he first turned out in the morning on his duties. Each morning the sentry on duty waited for the general's car to drive up to the château, and quickly warned me so that I had the whole guard ready for the important moment. As the general showed his nose outside the door of the château the sentry, at the top of his voice, bawled out, 'Guard – turn out.'

At the double we all raced to our positions and, dressing my guard in line and quickly seeing that rifles and equipment were in proper place, I waited for the appearance of the general, who sometimes strolled down the drive to inspect us, or drove very slowly past in his car as my voice roared out 'General salute – present arms.' A smile and a nod of appreciation from the general and the car moved off – another few moments of anxiety safely over. The only other occasion when the whole guard was turned out was when another general of the same rank as ours, or of a higher rank, came to visit the château.

For the first few days we kept a sharp look-out for a messenger from our battalion. We were anxious to know how they had fared in the attack. Then one came along. Eagerly I and the boys questioned him about the attack. Quickly came back the answer that the battalion had been cut up and he began to reel off names of officers and men he knew had been killed. I asked him how many sergeants had been done, and if Sergeant Faller had been one of them. Back came the reply without hesitation. 'Yes. Faller was blown to pieces the moment he got on top of the trench.' Silently I walked back into the tent. Poor old Faller. He certainly knew that his time had come.

Well, life on divisional guard was not bad at all; meals were not bad and came regularly. I was allowed to go off into the village for a few hours and leave my corporal in charge of the guard. Life was easy and pleasant during our six weeks guarding the general. But all good things must come to an end and one day along came a guard from another regiment to relieve us. We packed up our kit and once again marched off to join our own battalion.

Our luck was still good and we found the battalion resting behind the line in a burnt-out village. It was badly depleted; a lot of familiar faces were missing; and we soon learned of the terrible time we had fortunately missed. Here we lived for a while in the cellars or the rooms of the cottages that had missed the fire or only suffered slightly from the bombardment. Recruits began to join us to make up our strength, but they had only a very little training before being sent out to France and I, along with other officers and NCOs, had the task of making them somewhat fit for the trenches. Day after day I taught them the loading, handling and throwing of live bombs. Taking these recruits individually in a trench, we let them feel what a bomb was like when the safety pin was drawn.

My officer on these occasions usually discarded his tin hat, hating to wear the heavy things at any time. But he did this once too often. One particularly nervous recruit, after drawing the safety pin from the bomb, hit his hand on the back of the trench while trying to hurl it forward, the bomb dropping in the trench. Quickly in the few seconds left to me before it exploded I picked the bomb up and threw it quickly out of the trench, but even as it was in the air above the trench it exploded, scattering the metal all about. We had all ducked quickly but my officer had been too late, a fragment of bomb had ploughed a furrow across the skull of his uncovered head. Quickly I bandaged his head and sent for aid. He was quite conscious, and as he was being carried away on the stretcher he whispered to me, 'Don't forget, Sergeant, I was wearing my tin hat. It was knocked off in the dash for the bomb.' 'Sure, Sir,' I said, and another case of neglect of duty was kept a secret from those in command.

Once again orders came through to move, and we said goodbye to the broken and blackened walls of the village.

In June 1917 the 32nd Division took over the extreme left of the Allied line in the
Nieuport sector. The 16th Lancashire Fusiliers spent part of its time in the front line, a
particularly disagreeable spot which straddled the River Yser and its numerous canals,
and part resting further down the coast. Unpleasant though the Nieuport sector was, the
division's presence there meant that it missed the Third Battle of Ypres and one of the
grimmest episodes of the war, the struggle for Passchendaele ridge. It was not until
November 1917, when British offensive had at last died away, that Ashurst's battalion
moved to the northern part of the Ypres salient. It went into the line at Saint Julien – not
far from Mouse Trap Farm, where Ashurst had been gassed in May 1915 – on 27
November. The battalion stayed in the area, usually in the line in Houthulst Forest or
resting at camps in Pilckem or Boesinghe – for the remainder of 1917 and the first three
months of 1918.

Ashurst has in fact transposed the two moves, suggesting that his battalion went to
Ypres before it held the Nieuport sector. His battalion's calendar of moves, however,
confirms that Ashurst is in error.

Lots of new men had joined the battalion, and in something like fighting
strength again we were once more jolting along in the rattling old cattle-
trucks, then marching, marching, marching ever nearer some part of
that horrible front again – a front that had seen me twice before, and
where twice before also Fritz had seen to it that I had not got away scot-
free; a front also that every English and German soldier dreaded,
Passchendaele in the Ypres sector. What a battlefield! What a graveyard!
Miles and miles of land that had been churned over and over again by
both German and English guns; thousands and thousands of shell-holes
of varying sizes and depths, some full of water several feet deep.

As far as the eye could see the land was honeycombed; different tracks
to the front line could be picked out by the slippery duck-boards
zigzagging along the edge of the muddy craters. Here and there was a
break in the track where a shell had been directed at some ration party or
relieving party. Dirty white concrete pillboxes which had been built by
Fritz stood gaunt here and there as if defying the terrible explosions that
burst beside them. Lying about were wrecked gun carriages and ration
carts. Aeroplanes lay where they had fallen, burnt out, shot down in
flames by the enemy, or brought down in a fair fight for the mastery of
the front.

Pieces of equipment, damaged tin hats, bully beef tins, jam tins,
broken rifles and rusty bayonets, barbed wire and wiring stakes were
strewn about in the grey mud, one long desolate waste as far as the eye
could see, to the ridge in the far distance where at intervals a dirty black
smoke rose from the earth mingled with countless lumps of dirt, and
where tin-hatted grimy men pulled at dried fag-ends and uttered curses
and wishes not fit to be written. Hell itself would be nice and peaceful
compared with Passchendaele.

In the reserves we had halted; long shelters had been made in the wide trenches, and into these we threw our heavy kits. These were our homes again, for how long we had no idea, but it was not for many days. Our guides went off into the front line to get acquainted with it and know their way about. As soon as they had done that we packed up our kits again and moved off in the darkness. Like Indians, in single file we slithered along the duck-boards helping each other through the muddy patches where the boards had been blown apart. Quickly and quietly we carried on, getting a little breather while some poor fellow was pulled up the slippery side of a shell-hole into which he had fallen.

Great shells went humming over our heads, to crunch miles behind us, while whiz-bangs seemed to come straight at us as if the Germans could see us in the light of the many star lights that continually floated over no-man's-land and showed us each other's grotesque figures in the shimmering mud. Then suddenly a battery of our own guns behind us would let go a salvo of shells at Fritz; these passed over our heads like an express train. Bullets began to spatter about us now and as we advanced, still in the open, the ping of flying lead caused us to crouch down almost on all fours. The figures in front quickened their pace and a whispered order came from the front to split into sections.

At last we heard whispering a few yards ahead and then in front of us was a trench. Down into this we slid on the seats of our trousers. Quickly the relieved men helped each other on top of the trench and with barely time to wish us luck they vanished in the darkness. Soon we explored our little trench, which was no more than a straight hole in the ground about fifteen yards long and about six feet deep. One had to get out of the trench and walk along in the open twenty or thirty yards to reach the next platoon. It was more a line of outposts than a regular front-line trench. Fritz was entrenched similarly, three or four hundred yards away along a small ridge.

In the night rations had to be brought miles across the open, and getting them to us was a terrible and dangerous job. Each night sandbags full of precious rations had gone to the bottom of a flooded shell-hole with the man who carried them. Stone jars of rum wrapped in a sandbag were carried across that muddy waste, and when only a few yards from the trench every drop of the precious stuff was lost as a German bullet smashed the jar to pieces.

Three days and nights we had existed in this muddy hole, and I was peering over at Fritz's lines. The night was not too dark and I drew my officer's attention to moving figures just discernible on the ridge in front of us. Fritz seemed to be getting relieved or he was preparing for an attack. Thinking it was the latter, I fired at the figures. Others in the trench joined me and our officer ordered every man to stand to.

However, no attack came, but we must have done a little damage to

Fritz for when daylight came the Germans began a terrific bombardment of our trench. Great shells came thundering down on us. Fritz seemed intent on blowing us clean off the earth and I am sure that every one of us in those muddy outposts thought his last day had come. Every minute we expected the shelling to cease and the Germans to charge across at us, and in between the screaming shells we would quickly bob up our heads out of the trench and take a hurried look into no-man's-land. Into the sky we fired the SOS signal to our artillery and before it had fluttered down to earth the boys on the eighteen-pounders were giving Fritz as much as he gave.

Then out of the sky came a great shell, straight for us in our little trench. Instinctively I shouted 'Look out' and dropped to the bottom of the trench on my knees, hugging the dirty clay side as close as possible, but the next man to me ducked almost at the same time, throwing his body clean over mine. I felt the shell hit the earth and then the whole trench seemed to fall in on me. All went dark and I realised at once that I was buried alive. I could not move a limb, but I could breathe, the brim of my tin hat having prevented the earth from falling about my face.

I shouted at the top of my voice for help, at the same time trying to lift the heavy load from me, straining my back and using every ounce of my strength. I shouted again until I felt my strength going, and I was now breathing with difficulty. My chest ached. I was fully conscious of the hell that was outside my prison, and the thought that my comrades might be killed and I would lie there helpless, to die, took possession of me. Strangely, in that darkness, my mother, my father and my sisters and brothers all came to look at me, their faces fading away as I must have slipped into unconsciousness.

But my officer and men were not killed and had heard my shouts for help. In spite of that terrible shelling they gallantly dug like fiends to release me. When I regained my senses my eyes were looking up to the sky. I was released as yet only to my neck; my whole body was still fast. Shells were still falling about, powder smoke was everywhere, but how lovely and fresh the air tasted to me. Then, getting more used to my surroundings with the little liberty allowed me, I saw that there was a man's leg quite close to my face. It was the leg of my comrade who had ducked down over me, whose body had had the life blown clean out of it but which at the same time had shielded my body from a similar fate.

As the shelling died down and Fritz gave us a little respite the boys soon got to work again with the spades and I was dug clean out. My whole body was sore and I felt done. My face was bruised where the boys had striven to get air to me while I was buried. So I lay in the trench until darkness. Having regained a little strength I found I could just walk, and with the help of a comrade very painfully I made my way to the first dressing station, where I was examined by a doctor and then placed in a motor ambulance and taken further behind the lines.

My next stop was at a group of huts where men rested and recuperated for a week or two before being sent back up the line again to rejoin their units. I remained at this wooden camp for two weeks. We simply had food and shelter, neither of which was anything to swank about, and the only recreation was watching Chinese labour battalions making new roads.

These yellow chaps were the most sly and treacherous in France, and when not working they lived in compounds surrounded by barbed-wire fences. There was lots of trouble with them, and with a sly grin on their ugly faces these stockily built and miraculously strong Chinks would dance about the road with three or four sandbags of earth balanced on their heads. One day a party of them took a dislike to an officer in charge of them and while his back was turned one yellow fiend stuck a pick deep into the officer's back. Immediately they were rounded up by a battalion of Irish soldiers and driven into the compound, then machine gus were fixed around the barbed-wire fence. The guilty Chink was arrested and if quiet had not reigned in that compound those Chinks would have been mown down like wheat. Perhaps this treatment looked a little harsh, but drastic treatment was necessary with this wild, uncivilised crowd.[37]

My back was far from being well, but with some of the doctors at the front line one was malingering if one complained of any pain at all, and I was soon back again with my regiment in the line. When not in the front-line trenches we rested back in a reserve position, still amongst the shell-holes and mud, though we had the pleasure of little shelters made of sheets of corrugated iron thrown over a trench and camouflaged with a layer of mud. A couple of duck-boards made the floor, and a couple of men could just squeeze in and lie down.

During the daytime, while resting at these places, we had nothing to do but keep out of sight of enemy aircraft, sleep, smoke and lounge about. During the night there was work to do – hard and dangerous work. As soon as darkness settled on the front we set off up the line in parties, carrying heavy loads of sandbags, iron stakes, barbed wire and ammunition. Rain or snow, we slowly made our way to the front line, slipping, sliding, swearing, dragging one weary foot after the other out of the Flanders mud. Great, black shrapnel shells burst above our heads, spraying the rotten duck-boards with iron balls. Men groaned in their physical weakness, and called for help as they slipped into a great shell-hole and could not climb its slippery sides, or when they were struck with the hot metal of a bursting shell.

The stretcher bearers struggled alongside us, their muddy stretchers slung across their shoulders but ready to carry back across that muddy wilderness any man who could not walk for himself. Actually this supposed rest in the reserves was far worse than life in the front line itself. One night I went out in charge of a party of twenty-five men. It was necessary to go close up to the front line and we had almost completed the job when Fritz must have spotted us for suddenly shells came at us thick and fast and a machine gun peppered the ground all about us. Quickly we dashed for any cover to be found but from the shouts and groans of my men I knew that Fritz had got a few of them. Back to our little shelters we struggled, bringing the wounded with us and leaving two behind dead.

On arrival I reported to my company officer that I had seven casualties out of my party of twenty-five. 'Yes, Sergeant,' he said, 'I believe you have caught it pretty badly this trip.' He continued, 'There is still another lot of stuff to be taken up there and I am afraid you will have to make the journey again with another party.' 'Me?' I gasped. 'Yes,' said my CO. 'You know what a shortage of officers and NCOs there is.' 'I don't care what a shortage there is, Sir, I am not going up there again tonight,' I shouted angrily. 'It seems to me, Sir, that I have just to keep on going up there until Fritz does get me. But let me tell you that I have done my whack in this war, and if you consider this is mutiny, get on with the penalty, your revolver is handy. I might as well die nice and comfortable here in this little dug-out as up there in that hell hole.' 'All right, Sergeant,' said my CO, 'I shall report you to the colonel.' I walked away to my own little shelter.

My captain must have had a little sympathy in his heart for me for I heard no more about the affair. Once again we were too weak to be called a fighting battalion, and wearily we made our way behind the line, this time to regain our strength at a pleasant seaside town called Paris-Plage. Here we were billeted on the sand dunes in tents. The weather was nice and warm and in the mornings we could dash out of our tents clad only in an overcoat, trot down to the sea, discard the coat and bathe to our hearts' content. Some days while we were bathing an aeroplane would fly about over us, the pilot amusing himself by diving low, skimming the water, and making us dive below the surface, but we also enjoyed the fun.

We were allowed to go out in the town and enjoy ourselves to the full, and the boys made the best use of this privilege. Cooked meals, champagne, *vin blanc*, beer and coffee were the order of the day. Muddy trenches and dug-outs were forgotten for a few weeks and the boys soon began to feel the old fitness again. However, it was destined to be a long war and the inevitable order to pack up for duty in the line came round once again.

The last evening I spent in Paris-Plage was in the company of three other sergeants, enjoying ourselves in the kitchen of an estaminet we had mostly frequented during our stay there. We had made great friends of the owner and his family, and on this particular night we had lots of

francs to burn. Knowing that money was not of much account in the
trenches, and that it might be a long time before we could again have a
jolly time together, we were determined to have one last good fling.

We arranged for a feast to be prepared for us and dined and drank far
into the night. One by one we deliriously left the estaminet by the back
door. Just as I reached the back steps something seemed to hit me very
hard on the head. I fell down a few steps but did not feel any pain. Hours
afterwards the voices of some of my boys brought me to my senses. Early
that morning we were to move off to the line and to be absent from such
a parade was desertion, and the penalty death. However, the boys missed
me, and knowing quite well the estaminet I usually frequented they had
come out to look for me, finding me where I had lain for a few hours in
the pouring rain. While I lay wrapped in a couple of blankets sipping hot
tea, the boys were busy drying my clothes at the cookhouse and packing
my kit. Thanks to those good lads I was nicely ready and not feeling too
bad when the order came to fall in and move off.

That day, with our heavy packs, we did a march of over twenty miles.
The champagne must have done me good for I finished that march in my
proper place at the head of my platoon, and also for quite a long way I
had carried the rifle of a weaker comrade. We came to a halt on the
outskirts of Nieuport and were billeted in houses that were empty but in
very good condition. Air raids on the place were, of course, quite
frequent, and long-range shells also played havoc with it, but stray shells
and odd bombs did not trouble Tommy much when he had a
comfortable shelter to rest in.

Only a couple of days passed, however, and we moved in to the front
line crossing a bridge over the canal on which it was suicide to stay one
moment longer than was necessary. My company also had to cross a
swamp on duck-boards and then proceed up a communication trench
that Fritz could fire straight into. There were good trenches in the line,
however, and also good small concrete pillboxes. This front was fairly
hot and one had to be most careful when moving about. Night patrols
and listening posts went out every night, and working parties were busy
wiring and digging.

After a spell in the line we were relieved and dropped back into the
town. We were now living in a tunnel that ran through the middle of the
main street, a kind of covered-in communication trench which also
carried the telephone wires to the different fronts. Around went the
rumour that a big attack was about to be made on our front and that the
navy was to co-operate with us. Preparations on a big scale were certainly
being made; men and guns were concentrating on our front; stacks of
ammunition and other materials were about everywhere. New gas masks
were issued; field bandages and ammunition were examined.

The great advance was due to be made in a few days or so when

suddenly, without the least warning, Fritz opened a terrific bombardment on the town, also raining shells on the front line, the reserves, and
the new gun emplacements. We really thought that Fritz was forestalling
us with an attack, and the order came along for every man to be ready for
the line at once. Quickly and excitedly we strapped on our equipment,
fixed our gas masks in position for immediate use, and waited for the
order to move. Very soon the order came. My officer told me to take my
men and make for the portion of the front line we usually held. Shouting
out 'Come on, lads' off I went. At the end of the tunnel we dashed into
the open street. Shells seemed to be falling everywhere; bricks and slates
and glass were flying all over the place and the air was thick with dust
and powder smoke.

Aeroplanes roared high up in the sky dropping great bombs that
seemed to rend whole rows of buildings asunder. Our guns were barking
back at Fritz as fast as they could be loaded, and one could hardly hear
the shout of pain as some comrade was struck by the flying debris.
Madly we ran for the canal bridge, but awestricken we hesitated as salvo
after salvo came screaming about it. However, it had to be crossed, and
preparing ourselves for the mad dash we ran like frightened rabbits, not
feeling our heavy loads as we pictured in our minds those terrible shells
racing for us.

Once we were over the bridge the canal bank afforded some shelter,
and those who had safely made the crossing lay panting for breath as
their comrades still to come gained safety in twos and threes. Here I
checked my men and found that so far we had not done badly, only a
couple failing to show up. Our next move was across that terrible swamp
on the duck-boards, right in the open. I glanced over the bank to see how
the land lay in that direction. Shells were falling fast, churning up the
muddy swamp; the duck-board track was broken up in places, and
shrapnel balls were pit-patting into it like hailstones.

'We'll never get across there, Sergeant, its certain death to attempt it,'
said one of my men. 'Yes, so it is,' I said, 'but don't worry, we are not
going that way today. The fellow who ordered us to must come and take
us.' I led on along the canal bank under cover until I came to a
communication trench that would lead me to the front line. It certainly
took us longer to get there but it had saved most of our lives.

The front line was having a nasty time of it. Trenches had been blown
in in places and one had to dash across the open, risking the sniper's
bullet. Fritz kept up the bombardment and we crouched in the low
pillboxes. Some shells hit the top of them but the two feet of reinforced
concrete held and we just received a nasty, dull thud in our heads, or
when a shell burst near the entrance we felt the mighty draught through
our shelter.

Just one or two sentries were on duty outside crouching deep down in the trench and at intervals taking a quick glance over no-man's-land to see if Fritz was creeping up behind his barrage. But Fritz never came; he seemed quite satisfied to remain where he was.

For eighteen long hours the Germans kept up that terrible bombardment and when it died down he had done tremendous damage. He had smashed up trenches, guns and gun positions; flattened out reserve strongholds; inflicted heavy casualties; and instead of our being an army ready for the attack we were an army defeated and ready for relief. He had ruined the preparations of weeks and weeks. It was unbelievable. It was uncanny.

British plans for the 1917 offensive had indeed envisaged 'coastal and amphibious advances in the Nieuport – Ostend region'. These had initially been scheduled to start when the main offensive reached a point eight miles north of Passchendaele, or earlier if the Germans showed signs of great demoralisation (*Official History*, 1917, Vol. 2, p. 15). But preparations in this sector were, as the *Official History* admits, 'completely upset' by a German attack on the bridgehead north of the Yser in early July. German artillery and low-flying aircraft were particularly effective, and of the 1st Division's two forward battalions only 4 officers and 64 soldiers escaped. The Lancashire Fusiliers' history notes that the situation was worsened by the fact that 'No dug-outs of any strength could be made to protect the troops against the constant shelling'.

When relief did come along we retired behind the battered town of Nieuport to rest a while in tents. Rest, I said, but these resting periods close behind the line usually meant hard and dangerous work, and the front at Nieuport was no exception to the rule. On the morning of my first day out of the trenches I was summoned to my company commander's tent.

Our captain had been wounded in the bombardment and his place had been taken by a second-lieutenant, my own platoon officer, who was sat on a camp chair when I entered the tent. He looked at me rather stiffly and in quite an officious voice he said, 'I would like an explanation of your conduct, Sergeant, during the bombardment. I believe it took you quite a long time to get your men to the front line, and that you did not go the way you were ordered to. I want you to understand that that delay might have cost us our position in the line and to disobey orders like that can only be put down to cowardice, and I have a good mind to send you to the colonel.'

This little speech had taken my breath away. I stood speechless for a while glaring at him, then my blood boiled in me; horrible hatred burned my eyes; I cared nothing for differences of rank. I spat it out, 'You, you call me a coward! What a brave officer you are! What a lot of swank you've got when you are miles behind the line! Where were you while the bombardment was on? Why weren't you leading us the way to go? How did you get to the front line? Yes, take me to the colonel and I'll tell him how you have crouched in my dug-out while I and the boys have done your patrols for you, and enjoyed the stimulating effect of your whisky flask while we were doing them. Don't get so swell-headed because you are acting company commander. Don't forget we may have to go in the line again yet, and now I will go and tell all the boys what you have sent for me for'. Without a salute or anything I walked out of the tent.

Gathering most of my boys together I told them what had been said to me. There was a general chorus of angry curses and they wanted to go at once and see the colonel. What a lot of cowardice that officer would have had to answer for if I had only let those boys tell their tale to the colonel. Anyhow, a few days later we moved again for another front to the right of Nieuport, where our brave company commander sprained his ankle, or had the toothache or something and went down the line, sick.

Before going in the trenches on this new front the whole battalion were ordered on parade to listen to the adjutant read us a paper which had come from Army headquarters. I don't know how true the paper was, but it stated that the recent cutting up we had had at Nieuport in the bombardment was caused through the cowardice of a sergeant of a Welsh regiment who had been taken prisoner by the Germans. This sergeant had informed the Germans of our preparations for a huge attack, thinking that by selling his comrades he might save his own neck. Fritz, after seeing to it that our big push was a failure, kindly made it known to our authorities how they had learned of it, and by whom. What the eventual fate of this sergeant informer was I never knew.

For a few more weeks we kept going in and out of the trenches. The front was fairly quiet and it was a matter of staring across at Fritz's barbed wire and him staring at ours. Close behind our trenches flowed the canal in a deep cutting, and often on a nice day one would suddenly hear the roar of an aeroplane engine. To all appearances there was no plane about, until out of the cutting of the canal shot a small English fighting plane. Up into the sky it climbed and then over no-man's-land it gave an exhibition of aerial acrobatics seldom seen, twisting, twirling, skimming both our trenches and the Germans' by inches, the 'Mad Major', as the boys called him, leaning over the side of the cockpit and waving to us as he shot by at over one hundred miles an hour. Not a shot was fired at him; the Germans clapped their hands and laughed aloud at the comical and daring exhibition of aerial entertainment. A show both sides appreciated, a pleasant break from the monotony of trench life.

On 22 March 1918 the Germans opened a major offensive against the British south of Arras. The attack initially made good progress, inflicting heavy damage on the British Fifth Army. Troops were moved to the threatened sector, among them the 16th Lancashire Fusiliers, which was relieved in its trenches at Houthulst Forest, north of Ypres, on 27 March, and entrained for Savy, near Arras, the following day.

Soon, however, we were changing our front again. Actions were taking place further to the south, and fresh troops were needed there. Sometimes I think we did these long journeys from one front to another to bluff the German Command. Anyhow, it was a respite from the trenches, while jogging along in the old cattle-trucks, sleeping for a night in old barns or in some huge camp of canvas or wooden huts, not having any idea most of the time of what part of France we were in, or what part we were bound for, but always knowing that sooner or later we should arrive at some part of the front where another regiment was in need of a rest.

This time we landed where there was a little skirmishing coming off. Attacks and counter-attacks had been made until the real front line was hardly known. Nevertheless, after twenty-four hours in what was one of our foremost positions we were to advance to find where the German front line was, of which we were in some doubt. The barrage opened and off we went. There was not a lot of resistance and we had not many casualties. A small piece of shell skimmed my cheek, just scratching it. I hesitated, then ran on to a trench in front that was deserted until we got there.

The action ceased and we settled down to make the position secure in case Fritz decided to counter-attack, but no counter-attack came. The Germans shelled our new position a while and, so we thought, let us off lightly. Of course the work began now – digging, wiring, and strengthening trenches. Then in came our relief, while we fell back in the trenches in reserve.

7

Right Away to Blighty

While in the reserve trenches I was sent for by the colonel. When I presented myself before him his first question was, 'Sergeant, how would you like to go in for a commission?' For a moment I stared at him to make sure he wasn't joking. Then, thinking quickly I said, 'Oh, I can't be an officer, Sir, I haven't got any money. I couldn't keep the position up.' 'Nonsense, Sergeant,' said my CO. 'We don't want men of means as officers these days; we want men of experience like yourself – men who know this job and can lead others the way to go. Don't think about expenses, the government will see to it that you have all you require. I shall send your name forward to the general.' And, as though to show me that that was final, he started to write on some paper in front of him.

I saluted, wheeled about and returned to my men, whom I told of the colonel's offer. The boys soon convinced me that it was a glorious opportunity, and suggested that while I was away for my instruction the war might finish – a prophecy that proved to be true. A week later I was told to make myself presentable to be interviewed by the general.

After a lot of walking and a lift or two on ration and ammunition carts I arrived at the general's headquarters. After a while an orderly ushered me into the presence of the general. Wishing me good morning, he asked me a few things about myself – how long I had been an NCO, where and when I was promoted, and how long I had been out at the front, and if I had been wounded.

Standing strictly to attention I answered his questions quickly and smartly. Then he told me to relax and said that I was a fortunate young man, that I had done a great service already to my country, and that I was well deserving of a rest. He told me that he had visited the officers' training schools in England and that it would be absolutely my own fault if I did not enjoy myself there, adding, 'Don't forget to be a credit to your fine regiment.' With a 'Thank you, Sir' and a smart salute I took my leave of the general, the next thing being to find a place where I could have a good tuck-in before returning to my regiment.

However, the war was not finished yet. Our part of the front became very hot; each side was continually attacking and counter-attacking. On our right a French battalion was being hard pressed to hold a position they had captured from Fritz. We went over to assist them. The fields were strewn with dead Frenchmen, for their advance had cost them dearly and while what was left of them fell back we held their positions. Fritz tried hard to retake the trenches but we held on grimly, suffering heavy casualties but losing no ground.

More English troops came up a couple of days later and we once more fell back to the reserves amongst the French, with whom we did a good exchange in English cigarettes and French red wine. Behind this front we billeted out in an open field, using our groundsheets to lie on and pulling our overcoats over us in the night. It was summer time and quite warm and German planes came over frequently in the starry sky, dropping bombs and machine-gunning the earth below. We lay there trying to discern the enemy plane and watching tracer bullets shoot out from the machine, and listening to their hitting the ground around us, sincerely hoping that if one did hit us we should get it in the fleshy part of the leg – a nice Blighty wound. I had hardly rolled off my groundsheet one morning when I heard a messenger asking my whereabouts. I called him over to me and he said I had to report at once to the adjutant.

Away I went to headquarters, wondering what fresh instructions were being issued. I had hardly saluted when the adjutant gripped my hand and shook it hard. 'Congratulations, Sergeant,' he said, 'you are to proceed at once to England for your commission. Here are your instructions. You're a damn lucky fellow.' I took the papers he offered me. I couldn't speak for a moment. I felt rather queer. It seemed unbelievable that I could leave that horrible life of hardship and danger and go straight to England, safe and sound.

The adjutant's voice spoke again. 'Have you got any money?' 'No, Sir,' I said. 'Then take this', and he placed a twenty-franc note in my hand. 'You will need a little before you get to London.' 'Thank you very much, Sir. I only wish you all could come along with me,' I said. 'Well, get along while the going's good, and the best of luck to you, Sergeant.' I saluted and muttered, 'The same to you, Sir.'

I dashed back to the boys. One can only imagine the look on their faces when I told them the news. 'Right away to Blighty,' they seemed to keep saying to themselves over and over again. They helped me to pack my kit together and then with a heart mingled with joy and sorrow I bade them goodbye.

Off I went, marching easily down the country lane that summer's morning. My pack and rifle seemed quite light on my shoulders. My mind flew over to England and home, and then back again to the pals I had left behind me. Guns kept barking in the distance, and at intervals a shell would whine over my head. It was like a dream until a battery of our guns, hidden in the trees close by, suddenly barked out, wakening me with a shock.

It was rather warm walking along that dusty, country road, and I sat down for a while on the roadside, tasting the cool water from my water bottle and munching a hard biscuit. An aeroplane hummed overhead. I looked up fearing it might be a German and automatically looked round for a bit of cover in case he should drop a bomb or two in his attempt to find our guns.

I was not afraid. I just wanted to take a little extra precaution seeing that I was bound for Blighty. Anyhow, as the plane came into view I recognised the red, white and blue markings of our own aircraft. As I sat resting and watching the plane a motor lorry came bumping along the road going in my direction. I stepped into the road and motioned the driver to stop. 'Any chance of a lift, pal?' I enquired. 'Yes, jump up here. Where are you for?' said the driver. I told him the village I was going to and he enquired if I was going down the line sick, so I told him my real errand. 'Right away to Blighty,' he echoed. 'Phew, that's flattened me, kid. Jolly good luck to you.' Then, noticing me chewing biscuits, he asked if I had no bread. When I said I hadn't, he told me to dig my hand in a box under the seat and I should find some bread and cheese from which I could help myself. I had a very welcome ride with him for seven or eight miles, and then our ways parted and we said goodbye.

I had not far to go now to reach the place where I had to report. Here I joined two or three more from different regiments who were also going to England for a commission. We managed to get a decent feed and drink in the village and then the following day we were off again. Others joined us at different parts of the journey, and by the time we got to the boat there were twenty of us.

The senior NCO amongst us was in charge until we arrived in London, where a guide met us and directed us to Army Headquarters. Here we were interviewed separately, given a ticket to our homes, a pass for fourteen days' leave and £14 in cash, as well as an order to report at the officers' training camp at Ripon on the expiration of our leave.

This was my fourth visit to my home in about four years of war. I thoroughly enjoyed myself this time, not having to worry about going straight back to the front when it was over. Two jolly weeks over, and now to learn to be an officer.

I stepped out of the train at Ripon in Yorkshire, a pleasant little place with the ruins of a very old abbey close by. Spotting a soldier dressed rather neatly, with a narrow band of dark-blue ribbon around his hat, I guessed that he might be from the camp. I was right. He shook hands and welcomed me and as we walked towards the camp he explained life there, and in a few minutes I knew that what the general had told me in France was quite true. I was soon settled comfortably in a hut with about a dozen other fellows. Wounded officers, unfit for further service

139

abroad, were in charge of the camp, and gentlemen they were. Victoria Crosses, Distinguished Conduct Medals, Military Medals, and medals of valour from our Allies could be seen on the breasts of many men in the camp.

The routine was simple and the parades very easy. We had more privileges than the other troops who were camped round about us. The most severe penalty for doing wrong was known at RTU – Returned to Unit – which meant, of course, sent back to one's regiment in France. Any man who could not behave like a gentleman and conform to the simple rules of the camp certainly deserved RTU.

Life was surely pleasant at the camp after four years of shattered buildings and trenches in Flanders. I got along splendidly and passed my first tests easily, and I was waiting to go down to Cambridge to have the finishing polish put on me when on 11 November the whistles began to blow and the bells to ring. The war was over. Men danced about with delight; the WAACs who worked at the camp both laughed and cried. I didn't seem to get excited: the war had been over for me three months before.

It ended when I strolled down that long, dusty, French road saying to myself, 'Right away to Blighty.'

NOTES

1   The Special Reserve, formed in 1908 as part of R. B. Haldane's reorganisation of the army, was the descendant of the militia. It was tasked with finding drafts for regular battalions on active service, and its members were liable for service overseas. There were 74 battalions of Special Reserve in all, usually one for each battalion of line infantry, although the Lancashire Fusiliers had two. Battalions were based on the regimental depot, where recruits carried out their six months' basic training. Annual training was carried out by battalions under their own officers.

2   Veterans of the South African War, 1899 – 1902, identifiable as such by their medal ribbons.

3   Captain (later Lieutenant-Colonel) W. Lyle had joined the Special Reserve after leaving the regular army as a captain. He commanded the 3rd Battalion from April to October 1915, and was subsequently posted from the Lancashire Fusiliers to the 26th Battalion the Northumberland Fusiliers.

4   Ashurst joined C Company.

5   The procedure of stand-to, still used by the British army today, was designed to guard against attack at dawn and dusk. It also gave officers and NCOs the opportunity to check dispositions and equipment. Troops stood to under arms from shortly before first or last light until shortly after it.

6   The Regimental History of the Lancashire Fusiliers records that 'A Company played a football match against the enemy with an old tin for a ball: they won 3 – 2!' The best account of the Christmas truce is to be found in Malcolm Brown and Shirley Seaton, *Christmas Truce* (London, 1984).

7   Unlike the Germans, who were well provided with hand grenades, the British were initially forced to improvise. A common early device was the jam-tin bomb. The *Official History* (1915, Vol. 1, p. 7) tells its readers how to make one: 'Take a jam pot, fill it with shredded guncotton and tenpenny nails, mixed according to taste. Insert a No. 8 detonator and a short length of Bickford's fuze. Clay up the lid. Light with a match, pipe, cigar or cigarette, and throw for all you are worth.'

8   Probably the battalion's provost sergeant, rather than a member of the Corps of Military Police. Each battalion had its own provost sergeant, assisted by a small number of regimental policemen, responsible to the adjutant and regimental sergeant-major for discipline in barracks.

9   Griffin (awarded the DSO that February) was lightly wounded in the head as the battalion moved up from Vlamertinghe, and Captain J. E. S. Woodman assumed command. Griffin returned to duty shortly afterwards. Woodman was gassed at Second Ypres.

10   Ashurst was correct in surmising that his unit had got lost. Shortage of guides coupled with a lack of maps meant that B Company and part of C did indeed lose their way. The relief was not completed until 1.30 a.m. on 30 April.

11   Ashurst witnessed the attack of the Sirhind Brigade. The Gurkha battalion he saw was probably the 1st/4th Gurkha Rifles, on the right of the attacking brigade. It lost 58 men in the operation.

12   The Barn was in the grounds of Shell Trap Farm (later called Mouse Trap Farm), near Wieltje on the Ypres – Poelcappelle road. The battalion held an L-shaped position, with the farm at the angle. B Company, east of the farm, faced north, and D and A

My Bit

Companies, their trenches running north from the farm, faced east. C Company was in reserve just behind D and A. There was little in the way of a continuous trench, and there was no direct communication between B Company and the remainder of the battalion.

13 The German gas attack started at about 4.30 pm on 2 May.

14 Private J. Lynn, who had joined the 4th Battalion as a boy from the training ship *Exmouth* in 1901 at the age of 14½, commanded one of the battalion's four machine guns just north of the Wieltje – St Julien road. The machine-gunners, independent of the normal company chain of command and 'nobody's children', had not been issued with the primitive anti-gas protection that the rest of the battalion now had. Lynn opened fire into the gas cloud and, when he found that he could not longer see through it, he mounted his gun on a tree-stump on top of the bank near his position and fired wide traversing bursts into the gas and the German infantry behind it. He remained at his post until the attack had ceased, but was later carried off, literally blue with the effects of gas. He died in hospital the following day. Lynn had already been awarded the Distinguished Conduct Medal and the Russian Order of St George for bravery at Le Touquet. His final deed of heroism earned him the Victoria Cross, and Sir John French's despatch of 15 June 1915 carried a full description of the act.

The Lancashire Fusiliers suffered heavily in the battle. They had started the day with 33 officers and 1,070 men, and there were only 8 officers and 80 men in the line at the end of it. Many of those had been gassed and rejoined the battalion later.

15 Professor J. B. S. Haldane (1860 – 1936), an expert on the effects of gas in mining. He played a leading part in the search for an effective respirator, and visited France to see things for himself in April 1915. For a scholarly study of the use of gas in the First World War see L. F. Haber, *The Poisonous Cloud* (Oxford, 1986).

16 Possibly Mary, the American-born wife of Sir A. H. F. Paget.

17 The 3rd (Special Reserve) Battalion, which Ashurst had first joined, was stationed at Sutton Village near Hull. In November 1916 it moved to Thirtle Bridge, near Withernsea. It remained there till the end of the war, carrying out coast-defence duties and finding drafts for battalions in the field.

18 *Northland* (later renamed *Zeeland*) was a 17,905-ton vessel built by John Brown in 1901.

19 This vessel was in fact the RMS *Aragon*, headquarters of the lines of communication staff. They were notably unpopular, and it was unkindly suggested that 'at the end of the campaign *Aragon* was aground upon empty bottles as upon a coral-reef'. See John North, *Gallipoli: The Fading Vision* (London, 1966), p. 251.

20 Warships at anchor off the coast were particularly vulnerable to submarines, and Commander Hersing in U-21 sank the battleships *Triumph* and *Majestic*. He was later deceived into attacking a transport disguised, with wooden guns and superstructure, as the battlecruiser *Tiger* and learned of his mistake only when the superstructure floated away as the ship sank.

21 In fact this wiring was the work of the Royal Engineers Signal Service. The Corps of Signals was not formed till June 1920, and became the Royal Corps of Signals in August the same year.

22 *Southland*, with part of the 6th Australian Infantry Brigade embarked, had been torpedoed by U-14 thirty miles south of Lemnos on 2 September 1915.

23 On 25 April the converted collier *River Clyde*, with 2,000 troops aboard, was run aground off V Beach. The troops attempting to land from her, and those in accompanying lighters, suffered appalling casualties before eventually gaining a foothold ashore.

24 The final evacuation took place on 2 January 1916.

25 The Corps Commander (VIII Corps) was Lieutenant-General Sir Aylmer Hunter-Weston, universally known as 'Hunter-Bunter.' He had commanded the 29th Division in the Dardanelles. However, it is probable that Ashurst is referring to a visit to his

142

battalion by the divisional commander, Major-General (later General Sir) H. de B. de Lisle, on 29 June.

26   This was almost certainly one of the specially marked aeroplanes on contact patrol. There were two of these per corps, one using wireless and the other returning from the line to drop messages at corps headquarters. Their markings were intended to make them obvious to the advancing infantry, who were equipped with reflective squares of tin, attached to the backs of their packs, so that the aircraft would see them clearly. See *Official History*, 1916, Vol. 1, p. 297.

27   Lieutenant Geoffrey Malins, the official War Office cinematographer, filmed the Lancashire Fusiliers at about 6 on the morning of 1 July, before setting up his camera to film the explosion of the mine beneath the Hawthorn Redoubt. Malins gave an account of his exploits in *How I filmed the War* (London, 1922). Part of his material was used in the film *The Battle of the Somme*, although it seems certain that the film was at least partly reconstructed. See A. J. Peacock, 'The Somme Film – Some Notes', in *Gun Fire*, vol. 1, no. 1. One of the best-known still photographs of the Battle of the Somme shows the Lancashire Fusiliers fixing bayonets in the front-line trench. The warrant officer to the right foreground is Company Sergeant-Major Nelson of C Company. Officers were dressed like the men, and the officer to the rear of CSM Nelson has had to turn up the cuffs of his ill-fitting soldier's tunic. Both CSM Nelson and his company commander, Captain E. M. Dawson, were hit as they stood up to give the order to advance. The men of the two rear companies, C and A, carried an assortment of engineer stores in addition to their 120 rounds of ammunition, two days' rations and two bombs. The authenticity of this photograph has been generally accepted. George Ashurst suggests, however, that it was taken in late June, rather than on the morning of 1 July itself.

28   Two platoons of the 2nd Royal Fusiliers sprinted for the mine crater on Hawthorn Ridge, but the Germans beat them to it. The Fusiliers made several attempts to press on, and about 120 of them congregated at the crater. At about 9.45 there was what the Lancashire Fusiliers' War Diary calls 'a sudden retirement' amongst the troops to their right, either the Royal Fusiliers or a second-wave battalion, the 16th Middlesex. It was probably this withdrawal that Ashurst saw, and his battalion headquarters, too, feared that it indicated a German counter-attack. The 2nd Royal Fusiliers suffered 561 casualties that day, including their commanding officer.

29   A German heavy shell, so called from the black smoke of its explosion.

30   The 1st Battalion the King's Own Scottish Borderers, which had attacked south of Beaumont Hamel on 1 July, losing 20 officers and 548 men in the process.

31   All sources testify to the unpopularity of the Bull Ring at Étaples, where the harshness of the instructors – known, from their yellow arm-bands, as 'canaries' – was legendary. In September 1917 resentment flared into serious unrest. This is dealt with at length in William Allison and John Fairley, *The Monocled Mutineer* (London, 1978). However, some aspects of this account are unsatisfactory, at least in part because of the book's reliance upon the uncorroborated testimony of survivors. A BBC drama of the same name aroused considerable controversy.

32   German atrocities were certainly exaggerated by rumour. However, there is no doubt that the destruction which accompanied the German withdrawal to the Hindenburg Line had been carried out with a thoroughness which dismayed even some Germans: one of them left a sign reading 'Do not be angry: only wonder' in the ruins of Péronne. For a good account see E. L. Spears, *Prelude to Victory* (London, 1939).

33   The battalion was in reserve in the villages of Hombleux and Bacquencourt from 23 to 25 March, and at Douilly from 25 to 31 March.

34   Ashurst was correct in theory: the *Manual of Military Law* (1914) confirms that the death penalty could indeed be awarded to a soldier on active service who 'breaks into any house or other place in search of plunder'. In practice, though, no British soldier appears to have been executed for looting during the First World War. See Anthony Babington,

For the Sake of Example: Capital Courts-Martial 1914–20 (London, 1983). Had Ashurst and his partners in crime been apprehended and prosecuted, they would have been brought before a field general court martial, for the offence was too serious to be dealt with under the commanding officer's powers of jurisdiction. Reduction to the ranks and a prison sentence would have been the most likely punishment of the sergeants had they been convicted.

35   Major-General C. D. Shute commanded the 32nd Division from 19 February 1917 until 27 April 1918, with Major-General the Hon. A. R. Montagu-Stuart-Wortley commanding on a temporary basis between 24 May and 20 June 1917.

36   Sergeant Faller (the one pseudonym used in these memoirs) was killed in the attack on Savy Wood, an operation carried out by the 96th Infantry Brigade, which included the 15th and 16th Lancashire Fusiliers, on 1 April 1917. The 16th lost 5 officers and 119 men in the action.

37   Large numbers of Chinese were recruited for labouring duties in France. There were some problems with discipline, the most serious being the mutiny of No. 74 Labour Company at Boulogne, which downed tools and went on the rampage: 27 of its members were shot dead and 39 were wounded. See Michael Summerskill, *China on the Western Front* (London, 1982). The often forgotten contribution made by Chinese labourers in British rear areas is commemorated by the distinctive headstones marking the graves of those who died.